Grave Misconception

Felicity Snowden

In memory of the brave men and women

who tragically lost their lives on board HMS Rohilla

-Saltwick Nab, Whitby on Friday 3oth October 1914.

“How blessed are some people, whose lives have no fears, no dreads; to whom sleep is a blessing that comes nightly, and brings nothing but sweet dreams.”

Bram Stoker

ACKNOWLEDGEMENTS

I'd like to thank the following people for their help and support in the writing of this book:

Proof Reader – Andie Musson

Literary Advisor – Sue Stocks

IT Support - Allison Ward, Dawn Leak

Beta-readers - Mark Atkinson, Carol Haigh, Mike Bailey, Kath Mc Donald

I am also most grateful to Heather Sheldrick from 'Now, Then' folk group, Barnoldswick and Earby- who kindly allowed the use of lyrics from the poignant and captivating track commemorating the Rohilla tragedy.

Finally to my husband, Vic for his endless patience and encouragement.

Annette McBride's Family Tree

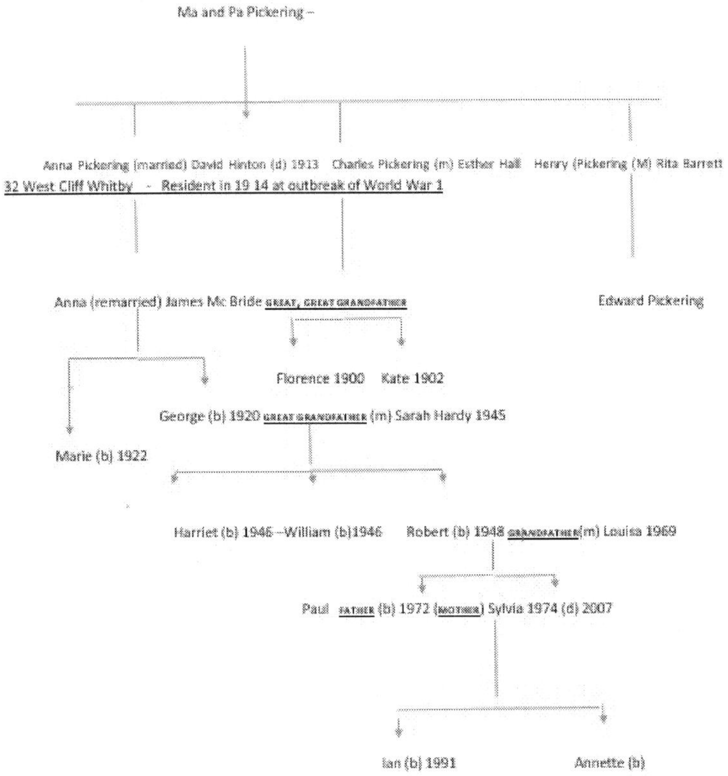

CHAPTER 1 Lou's Story – 2014

Lids wide open and eyes staring, Lou scanned the ceiling. Breath steady, senses sharpened, body in alert mode. Something stirred below, fluky for this time of the morning and definitely worrying.

The hangover head swivelled taking in the digital seven thirty, as pages of the 'Classic Racer' supplement fluttered fanlike to the floor. A fresh wave of nausea engulfed him. He cringed as a chair scraped the tiled floor, reverberating mercilessly on his suffering scull. Who or what was down there?

A distant shuffling sound, followed by a clatter as though every piece of cherished china had hit the deck. Instantly Lou was sitting up, rigid against the velour headboard a cushion for the pounding head as he gripped the heaving stomach. His sister, Ellie wouldn't be up and about at this time, judging by her late return last night and she rarely emerged before ten, even on weekdays.

And yet it was a saga he'd heard before, a repeat performance, he told himself. Fears diminished he sank back into the Memory Foam in recall.

A constricted cry emanated through the house, bringing a wry grin to Lou's face as he reached for the water glass. Gulping a generous mouthful to relieve the dry, dehydrated feel, he returned to recovery position. A voice exploded in his head.

"That beast's loose again……"

Though his pain was torturous, Lou's eyes glistened with relish. For a second he savoured the moment, ears cocked for a further instalment. He didn't have to wait long either.

"Lou, did you hear me?"

It wasn't difficult to imagine him panting, perpendicular against the kitchen wall, hardly daring to move an inch in either direction, pupils darting here and there like a spectator at a tennis match. The big hands trembling, brow spotted with neat little beads of sweat, his lip quivering.

What a wimp, Lou thought. Of all the haunting locations, the gruesome guises and sinister plots he'd handled in his career and every time he managed to lose it. This was a pet snake after all, not a man eating tiger. He was pathetic.

Somewhere upstairs a door creaked, maybe Ellie tripping to the bathroom as the landing light flicked on. Then for a moment, silence before the rumpus began again.

A scurry of footsteps across the kitchen, a squawk from the cat as Lou envisaged his dash for the door. A click of keys retrieved from the hall table told him his father was leaving `post haste', the letter flap sounding a final farewell.

Out in the street, courage returned and the dialogue continued.

"Sort it, Lou….I'll be back before closing time."

Despite the heavy head, the tiresome task of capturing the 'beast' and securing him safely in the vivarium Lou managed to devour the bacon butty Ellie prepared for him at breakfast. He groaned disapprovingly between mouthfuls catching snatches of his sister's conversation with her school chum, Lisa as they discussed their planned shopping trip.

Why did she take so long on these occasions? Swanning in and out of the same shops, comparing price tags, waiting in the longest checkout queues.

He swigged the much needed black coffee contemplating the morning ahead, whilst waiting for the inevitable text.

Ping…there it was. He put off reading it, knew already what it would say…. Hadn't he read it a thousand time before?

Lingering by the mirror Ellie applied the final touches to her make- up, the phone wedged 'twixt ear and shoulder. Applying mascara as she listened and pausing at intervals she uttered affirmatives.

She was a tall, slender, blonde with a pale complexion and striking features mounted on a heart shaped face. The bright hazel eyes were her best feature though, tantalising, sparkling, beneath the long silky lashes. Her wardrobe was uncomplicated, consisting mainly of faded denims and skimpy T-shirts which hugged her enviable figure with ease.

"Yes, yes," she said. "I'll be there, Lisa…. 11 o'clock outside Next."

Lou reached down grimacing, the pain still circulating his temples and read the text.

"Don't forget Ellie today, Mum x"

He wasn't going to get out of this one in a hurry that was plain…. and then there was tonight's little escapade, an all-night shindig, at Lisa's. Was there no end to it?

His stomach lurched again, in response to the bacon butty and he reassembled his thoughts. He had intended to watch the motor cross, pamper the python and then down a few beers. Just another wasted day playing nursemaid to the kid sister. True she was vulnerable, every teenager is...but if Ellie weren't so needy, so naïve...if she wasn't his sister. How come he always got landed?

It wasn't the hangover that plagued him most now but the thought of his forthcoming chaperone duties. Lou was angry, he blamed his Dad of course. He was the parent, Ellie was his responsibility. He was the root of all Lou's troubles, nothing seemed to go right from the minute he'd been born.

All the endless days and nights spent home alone, he and Ellie like veritable orphans pushed from pillar to post while their parents worked all hours. If it hadn't been for Aunt May their kindly neighbour who'd stepped in, filled the void, Lou dreaded to think what would have become of them.

And now at twenty one, two failed college courses, a string of short lived relationships, not to mention Suzie. Lou choked up momentarily, lingering on her memory as Ellie shouted from the hallway.

"Lou, get a move on ...we'll be late!"

'Suzie', he sighed to himself as he grabbed his coat. Beautiful, intelligent, fun loving Suzie. Nothing seemed to go right since Suzie.

Lou stood in the alcove watching the proceedings. The room was dimly lit with little glimmering candles strategically placed on tables next to ramekins full of nuts and crisps. The latest Pharrell Williams song blurted from the music dock as a number of semi naked females floated drunkenly between cavorting couples. The party was in full swing, Lisa's parents were away and she was certainly making the most of it.

Eleven thirty and it was Lou's task to steer his sister toward the door. He'd called a taxi for midnight but through the excitable throng he noticed Ellie's long term boyfriend had eventually arrived. This could spell disaster and Lou would have to work quickly if he were to meet the Cinderella deadline. A moments delay and Ellie would be entrenched in his sickly embrace, irretrievable, his early escape plan doomed.

Lou watched the striking newcomer slip easily into the crowd, pinching gyrating bottoms in his path as he weaved his way through the packed hallway, a grunted greeting to his beer swigging buddies. The olive complexion and strong features instantly demanding attention. But the main allure seemed to be the beady eyed creature perched perilously on his left shoulder. A squawking minor bird, his piercing tone in direct competition with the strains of the more appealing Pharrell William's track.

The strange pair hesitated by the kitchen door, instantly attracting more female company, including that of his sister. Lou had absolutely no idea why; he was a complete low life, totally weird and utterly selfish.

Richard Etchington, nick name 'Retch' was a hopeless drop out but Ellie worshipped him. It had been some time before Lou had realised the implications of the spelling, of course. He'd lost count of the projectile vomiting displays he'd witnessed following his heavy drinking sessions. But now recalling past parties, Lou relaxed, secure in the knowledge that he'd shortly be out cold.

Ellie sought him out wrapping her slender arms around his broad shoulders before relieving him of his faded jacket. Eyes piercing and prying he took in the occupants of the room in a swift glance. His smile was not for Ellie though, but for his host who indicated the extravagant array of alcohol lined up on the kitchen worktop.

"Rum and Coke!" screeched the bird. "Scotch on the Rocks!"

Silenced with a flick of his wrist, the bird flew protesting to the safety of the curtain rail as Retch homed in on the ample booze.

Lou reckoned he'd had a skin full already. Just one more whisky and with the obnoxious contents of his stomach duly expelled, he and Ellie could slip away.

When was he going to be released from this ordeal? Was there no end to his overseeing duties?

It was all his father's fault. If he wasn't so wrapped up in his oh so vital occupation if he'd bothered to spare time for their birthdays, Christmas nativities, parties, and family holidays. If he'd even acknowledged their existence. Oh, he'd managed to drop in for five minutes apparently when Lou had been christened.

'I name this child Lucien Peter Bannister'. Lucien….he'd heard all the gags of course, Lucy, Lewd, Ludicrous. The truth was far more startling of course. Centred round the box office successes of the time, the Peter Cushing's and Christopher Lees' of the production era and their reverie with the devil. Lucifer. Why not just settle for that, though Lou.

Pondering on these thoughts a wave of anger engulfed him, colour flooding his cheeks. He loosened his top button in response to the rising temperature and slipped further into the window recess.

The mobile reverberated in his pocket, unheard but persistent. Breaking from his trance he fumbled for the devise as he stumbled headlong into a couple of revellers in a clinch behind the door. His clumsiness failing to have an effect they continued petting, as Lou skirted the pair and made for the hall.

"Yeah," he bellowed above the din. "I'm hearing you!"

Outside on the moonlit drive Lou pulled his collar up toward his ears in a vain attempt to shield himself from the cold. His breath rose in little clouds, his voice suddenly loud in the silence of the night.

"Yeah," he said. "Next weekend, I know."

Lou listened, that restrictive feeling creeping through his bones, keeping his feet in shackles, his tongue controlled. He checked his watch, reflecting on the delayed departure, desperately looking for a loophole.

"I heard you. Six thirty at yours…I'll be there."

Lou sighed heavily replacing the mobile in his pocket. It was the Goth weekend at Whitby, there'd be a whole crowd there, strutting their stuff, filling their faces and getting in the beers. Seemed like the perfect escape but how would he achieve it with his sister in tow. If only he could make the break, give Aunt May the slip, fob off the old man and convince Ellie. He had to fix it somehow.

"We'll be down in the old town," Kalen was saying. "My uncle's got a place there…steeped in history, perfect, just perfect."

Kalen's athletic anatomy filled the doorway, standing a full six foot, his dark expressive eyes, cascading locks and the striking voice that never failed to impress. Male or female they stood in awe of his magnitude, self- assurance and downright good looks.

Lou followed Kalen into the living room, for once unmoved by his old school chums charms; he'd other things on his mind.

"Start out round two I'd say, stop at the ' Four All's' for a burger, then bomb it down to Whitby.

Lou yawned in response and removing the dog hair flopped down in the nearest chair. He'd been there dozens of times, the lingering smell of newly polished furniture, a hint of tobacco and the stylish but rigid settee. A little dated for the 21st century but with a certain 90's charm. His eyes closed instantly. He was feeling a little spaced out, the early morning journey home in the taxi having affected his stomach again; mainly this time through lack of sustenance and a few too many cokes. He'd managed to get to bed for five thirty, woken almost immediately by the infuriating ritual of the burglar alarm next door

"Lou, are you with me?" Kalen persisted.

Before he could respond the moulting mutt appeared, springing onto Lou's lap, the rough tongue scouring his familiar face, tail wagging excitedly. With a start Lou sat bolt upright, stroking the soft fur and patting him vigorously.

"Get off, Rufus!"

Kalen grabbed the ageing Lab by the collar, removing him swiftly from the room and slamming the adjoining door. His patience was running thin, the amiable smile that had greeted Lou on his arrival was fading rapidly. He paced the floor. Now a single shake of the raven head stirred the sleek tresses into motion, like the tide gushing forth in tune with his changing emotions.

"Sorry Kale, "Lou groaned. "Had a bit of a lousy night."

A pitiful whining sound emerged from the kitchen diluting the impact of the conversation. Kalen detested competition at the best of times and he strode over to the dividing door and kicked it with a passion.

"Shut up, you mangy mongrel."

As the whining continued Kalen grabbed Lou's arm roughly, prising him from the settee and dragging him toward the hallway. His feet were reluctant but Kalen was not easily deterred and if words would not win his friend's interest then it was time for a change of tactics.

He'd known Lou long enough to know what made him tick, what really motivated him.

It was pitch black in the garage. A stench of stale oil lingered there and Lou shuddered, a cool rush of wind spiralling his ankles as they entered. Only a thin horizontal strip beneath the double doors offered any form of light and Lou felt a sudden chill in the depth of his bones. He hovered uncertainly in the gloom as the adjoining door clicked shut, leaving only a slither of light to guide their way.

Kalen liked his melodramas, revelling in the mysterious, living on the edge. He was silent, relishing the darkness, ingesting the fumes, listening to the faint scuffling sounds. It seemed an age, though it was barely a second before he flicked the switch.

"With me now, Lou?" Kalen's smile flashed triumphantly before him. Suddenly Lou was wide awake, waiting on Kalen's every word, alert and intrigued.

In the centre of the double garage was an elegant Daimler, its highly polished surface gleaming in the beam from the overhead light. Kalen's father certainly had taste, together with the necessary income to indulge in his passion. Lou moved slowly round the pristine chassis, his hands skimming the surface, cooing with admiration.

"Don't stall, Lou."

Within seconds they were beyond the shining status symbol, taking in a smaller but no less desirable piece of machinery, a Vincent 1000 cc, again a classic and with undeniable appeal. Lou gasped open mouthed, completely lost for words as Kalen stood aside to savour the moment. He'd finally hit the target, snared the rabbit, hooked the eel, triumph shining from the very depth of his being.

"Hey, Kale….this is something else, where d' you get it?" Lou asked.

Kalen remained mute, arms folded in homage as if marking the occasion. Slowly he advanced mirroring Lou's earlier apathy with a similar hesitation.

"Like it?" he asked.

The smooth bodywork, fine detail, dashboard, headlights, and trims, its magnificence muted only by a layer of fine dust. Everything in place, everything immaculate and everything he'd ever dreamed about.

"Roadworthy?" Lou asked.

"Naturally."

"Taxed… tested?"

Kalen grinned from ear to ear as Lou grasped the handlebars firmly in his capable hands, nodding profusely. He raised his eyebrows, waiting for the next question, the one he knew would follow.

"When can I ride her?"

A certain disappointment crept over Kalen's face as he relayed the plans for the weekend. Lou would get some insurance, fill up with fuel and ride his dream machine to Whitby. It was the only way he could guarantee that Lou would be there, of course but a change to the original plan of action. It seemed there was only one person who could dictate to the indomitable Kalen, a force he'd never dare to challenge, a non-contestable element in his life and that was his father. On his last trip Kalen had been riding full throttle, misjudged a bend, incurred a speeding ticket and had his licence revoked for six months. His Dad had handled the police, paid the fine, but insisted that under no circumstances should Kalen attempt to ride the 'Vincent' for the foreseeable future.

"You're kidding?" Lou said.

Lou's sympathetic side surfaced, but it was short lived.

"I'll sort the insurance today, shouldn't be a problem, dust down the leathers and fill her up. It's a doddle."

Lou straddled the seat enthusiastically, flexing the hand brake, adjusting the side view mirror. He could almost hear the roar of the engine, feel the wind in his hair, and taste the salt air.

This was unbelievable, what luck. When he passed his test some months ago he never thought he'd ever actually take to the road. Fantastic, absolutely bloody fantastic.

Within a moment however Lou realised it was only a dream. Had he forgotten his more pressing engagement? The nightmare he lived with daily?

Releasing his hold on the handle bars he slid his leg back over the chassis, sighing deeply.

"Hold it Kale," he said. "It's not goanna' happen."

Kalen's hostile glance revealed a hint of the darker side to his personality that Lou had witnessed before. It was a momentary phase passing as quickly as it had arrived but Lou became guarded. He stepped back from the dream machine, mad with desire yet doomed to remain in his real but restricted world. There was just no way and he knew it. Ellie's welfare came first in his life and there wasn't a hope in hell he'd get her to ride pillion - let alone leave her loathsome lover.

"Don't be so hasty, Lou."

The smile reregistered on Kalen's face as he moved toward a small room to the rear of the garage. Here the atmosphere changed once more, the cold damp air returning and a putrid stench that Lou just couldn't place. Kalen located the switch but the bulb blew leaving the little room in complete darkness. Not to be deterred he fished in his pocket for a flashlight. There on the concrete floor stood a huge, ornate box instantly recognisable by its shape and fittings as a coffin.

"Holy smoke!"

"Impressive, wouldn't you say?" Kalen chortled.

It was a sickly laughter that emerged from his lips as he ran the spotlight over the exquisite surface.

"Someone died, Kale?" enquired Lou

"No …."

"Then what….?"

The glare of the flashlight hit Lou's horrified features, causing him to flinch. He shielded his eyes as Kalen threw back his head and rocked with a laughter.

"Look a little closer, Lou."

The casket glowed with a kind of ethereal beauty, its sculpted oak surface and ornate brass plaque a credit to the craftsman. Although Lou was aware of Kalen's family links with the funeral trade, he was at a loss to understand why the casket had been stored here in the family garage.

Lou's just couldn't make the connection….if no one had died, then what?

In all the years Lou had known Kalen he had always been just one step ahead, a planner, an achiever, leader of the pack. He'd learnt from experience that when he was around, just about everything was possible.

A cool smile slid across his face, a glimmer of hope rising. He hadn't noticed the set of wheels, propped up in the corner. Kalen wiped the surface of the casket, dust particles rising as he released the catch, revealing the internal seating.

"The axles' in need of some additional parts, suspension requires attention but they'll start work on her tomorrow," Kalen hovered over the frame. "It'll be ready for sure by Friday."

So, they were all set now, Kalen had done it again, thought of everything as usual, considered all the obstacles and made a faultless plan.

Now all Lou needed was to sort the minor details, pacify the parents and convince Ellie.

In short he needed to perform a miracle.

"You have to be kidding, Lou," Ellie was saying. "If you think I'm spending my week end with that crazy bunch, you've another thing coming."

Ellie, as usual was stubborn, abusive and Lou resented the way she always judged his friends. Yes, the Goths appeared a little scary, menacing even but under the surface they were human, skin and bone, just like us. Passive thoughtful people, with a feel for justice.

What did Ellie know anyway? And how could she describe the Goths as a 'crazy bunch' when she spent every waking hour with that idle cretin.

It hadn't been a good day so far. The weather was getting worse by the minute, the insurance quotes were extortionate and now as he knew she would, Ellie was giving him a hard time.

"Anyway, who'll take care of Butch? You said yourself he needs handling every day…."

"Besides Retch wants me down at the club, he's watching the band, getting in the beers," she continued her argument with gusto, no compromise, a fire in the hazel eyes.

Huh, getting the beers in….that would be the day, when he put his hand in his pocket. Biting his tongue, Lou sought a new angle, an irresistible draw.

"Hold on, who'll take care of Butch?" she asked. "You said yourself he needs handling every day…."

She was right of course, snakes who were rarely pampered could easily turn vicious. Aunt May, was quite capable, totally fearless and most times willing, but wasn't it quite short notice?

"And anyway, when does this set of psycho's actually hit the road?

"Lou paying little attention, found his mobile and flashed down his contacts, A.M, Aunt May.

"So…. what about Midnight?" he asked absentmindedly.

This wasn't an estimated leaving time but a reference to the other love in Ellie's life, her adored cat, Midnight. Born at twelve o'clock on Halloween the kitten had emerald green eyes, a black velvety coat and due to the current alignment of her stars she had undeniable, magical powers.

"It's not an issue, Lou. If I go, then she goes too!"

There was a certain sense of decision in the air now, though not without compromise. Ellie would be persuaded, if Midnight were included and if Retch agreed to drive down later in the old V.W. Now all Lou needed to do was sort the finer details. Babysitting Butch was not high on Aunt May's list of "must do's" for the weekend but after watching the supply of live baby mice running frantically around the adjoining cage and following a practice run of the feeding and handling routines, Aunt May agreed.

Lou packed a bag wondering how on earth he was going to deal with his parents. His dad was working on a new script and wouldn't be home till well after midnight and mum never arrived home before three a.m. He'd filled out somewhat since the time he'd worn the leather gear, bombing down to Brighton with Kalen for the festival, he'd ridden pillion, braving the October temperatures and ignoring the triple figures displayed on the speedometer. He shrugged, digging out his helmet and gloves and then paid the insurance online.

Meanwhile Ellie called Retch, the simpering voice a little overdone Lou thought. After several minutes she stopped her bleating and flipped over the iPod lid, banging it down on the table. The lip came out, recalling memories of an uneasy childhood, the unpredictable days, the lonely nights. Lou felt the lump rise in his throat then checked himself, before the sympathy flooded in.

"It's sorted, Lou," she mumbled, retrieving her handbag from behind the door. "He'll come over Saturday morning directly after breakfast."

Once the hangover had worn off, she meant. That would be sometime after supper no doubt and only under sufferance. Lou assumed he would be glad to spend some time away from that dingy pad he lived in. Packed between the bookies and the off licence a sordid little room above the laundrette, strewn with empty lager cans and take away boxes, it reeked of stale curry. Last time Lou had been there he'd been attacked by his manic bird and struggled to find a seat that wasn't splattered with crusted droppings.

"You packed?" Lou asked. "Promised Kalen we'd meet up at the pub midday……I'll check the wheels and we can be off."

Ellie left the room without a word, the pet lip still evident, acute resentment shadowing her face.

Why was she always so ungrateful? Wasn't it time she spread her wings a little, made new friends….ditched some of the old ones?

It was past ten when Ellie stepped out the front door, her overnight case in one hand, the pet carrier in the other. She put them down on the top step, turning to lock the door.

"Come on…" Lou called.

His patience starting to run out he reached for his helmet urgently flexing the throttle, the time was slipping by and the lads weren't prone to hanging around. They'd stretch their legs, stop for a fag then hit the road again.

Above the roar of the engine, Ellie let out a scream.

"What the hell is that?"

She left the luggage on the doorstep, a civet cry arising from the abandoned cage as she scurried to check out the sidecar. Waving her arms frantically, shaking her head in disbelief she waited for Lou to kill the engine. The promise of a long, lazy weekend at the seaside suddenly turning into a nightmare.

As the bike shuddered and stilled Lou glared at his sister.

"What's got into you……it's only a sidecar," he snarled. "Get in or we'll be late."

Lou could feel the heat rising from his collar, flooding his face as a streak of sweat meandered down is forehead. Drat it! He knew full well they'd never make it now, without running it off the clock.

With just a mile to go the weather was turning, a squally rain splattered their faces, the chaffing wind making them even more uncomfortable. God knows if it was like this inland, what would it be like on the coast? Lou blinked, wishing he had acquired some goggles.

Ellie was moaning again and Midnight could be heard whining pitifully, above the engines drone. Somewhere in the claustrophobic confines of the car the frantic animal was trying desperately to escape. This was turning out to be a complete and utter disaster, thought Lou and he was in half a mind to turn back now.

Hold on though, it hadn't actually been a doddle recruiting Aunt May on the snake sitting scheme and drafting the letter to Dad had been even worse. To be fair, it wasn't the first time he'd stretched the truth in order to gain a little freedom, do his own thing, be himself for a change. Lou hoped the line was convincing. The yarn about the interview on the coast, the prospect of a job in the shipping industry.

'Taking Ellie, just for the ride and left instructions on snake care with Aunt May. Keep you updated,' it concluded.

He was so gullible at times, his dad. Or was it that he just didn't care?

Lou was passed worrying these days, after all he was over the age of consent, a grown man and once he had secured a position he would be totally independent. He didn't need them, they didn't need him…..it was time he flew the nest.

The smell of burning rubber hit their nostrils, followed by a screech of brakes as they pulled into the car park. Lou's foot hit the ground scattering the loose gravel as he came to an abrupt halt beside the weather beaten inn.

"Thank God for that," sighed Ellie. "I thought I was goanna' die."

Why did girls have to be so pathetic? Lou frowned. He unfastened his helmet and secured the footbrake.

"Let's get inside before we freeze."

The forecourt was empty, no wonder - it wasn't exactly the Ritz. The grey looking exterior was hardly inviting either, as they dodged the hopscotch of puddles leading to the entrance.

Now he hesitated again. It had been almost three years since their last meeting, the perfect mix of eccentricities, picked by the top talent scouts in the country and fashioned to meet the changing demands of the commercial film market. Whatever Lou thought about his father, he was at least a perfectionist, a true master of his trade. Nothing short of sheer genius.

And the friendships established on the film set had endured and matured, well outliving the box office success; trips to the coast, numerous punk concerts, not to mention the regular beer binges. Surely nothing had changed, Lou told himself as he wiped his boots determinedly on the doormat and pushed open the swing doors.

Thankfully the bar was warm and welcoming, with a huge open fire and a friendly landlord. Mostly frequented by locals dressed in work overalls and a few tourists on their way to the coast it attracted a lively lunchtime crowd. Lou made for the bar and ordered two cokes.

"Well, look what the winds blown in, Merle", if it isn't young Lucy…"

Lou turned and a broad smile slid across his lips. In an instant he was in the intense grip of a bear hug that threatened to squeeze the life out of him. Released he stood back in awe at the giant that stood before him. Grinning he shook the outstretched hand, as the wise engaging eyes met his. The yellow mop of hair tied back a band now had a tell-tale grey steak but the physique was the same, his rippling muscles a reminder of the mere strength of the man.

"It's been an age Lucy…..and how's our little Ellie, still single?" he roared with laughter.

A tear sprang to Lou's eye, an emotional response to the meeting. This hunk of a man had always been the guiding light behind the group, the head and the heart, the genuine Godfather. Kalen was the mast head but it was Hathus that had the final word. He'd always been there, a shoulder to cry on an uplifting word when you were down, someone you could trust with your deepest secrets.

“I was just saying to my Merle how it was time we were all together again, a breath of sea air and a dram at the Griffin. It’s been too long.”

Out of the shadows his long term girlfriend appeared, dark locks framing the sensitive features, the silky black top and dark jeans hugging the petit figure. The years between them blindingly obvious but somehow unimportant. They were devoted and inseparable.

The greetings weren’t finished though as a slender, red hcad appeared loud and bustling in leathered pants and studded jacket.

“Perdy….” Ellie called.” Didn’t think you’d be here.”

She joined the group, her sexy voice and slinky outfit causing a stir with the lunchtime locals as she hugged Ellie tightly. They’d hit it off before, slipping of the set for a secret cigarette, raiding the perfume stores and chatting up the lads. Ellie’s previous disillusion with the trip seemed to have vanished in an instant as they struck up a heated conversation about the next level of Candy Crush.

Lou sighed. The long awaited meeting seemed to go like a dream. Just a collection of diverse yet likeminded young people, each ensconced in their own unique worlds, divided by distance yet united for all time by those enduring bonds.

Lou soon became restless and furthermore he was aware that they still had some miles to cover. While Ellie headed for the Ladies he checked their destination on the satnav, and paid the bill. The steak and kidney pie was giving him some discomfort as he strode out into the car park, wincing he clutched his chest as the acid resurfaced. And just his luck there was still no let- up in the weather.

As he turned the corner of the building, deep in though he was suddenly aware of someone hovering close to the bike, a tall hooded figure momentarily obscured by the dividing fence. Lou lunged forward, immediately on his guard.

“Hey, Scrote take your hands off,” he hollered.

The youth turned. He didn’t run as Lou had expected but remained fixed to the spot, a bold smile unfolding instantly on the untimely tanned face. There was just a moment before he spoke.

“Always on your guard Lou……nothing changes much then.”

Lou’s face lit up instantly, taking in the familiar figure he threw his arms around him with a mixture of relief and a recollection of times gone by. The sabotaging of Rigby’s lunchbox, the hoax fire alarm and best of all the snaring of Gina Waddington in the sixth form girl’s toilets. Those were the days.

The pair parted standing at arm's length, each holding council on the vivid recall.

"Gaz, what the devil you doing here?" Lou stuttered.

"Driving back to Whitby, Mate," he said. "Just flew into Manchester this morning."

The rain had ceased at last and Lou noticed the sporty Mazda parked to the rear, bodywork glinting in the first of the sun's rays. Garry Quilon had done well for himself, talented and quite academic as he remembered, parents loaded to boot. Well, we can't all have brains and brass, Lou supposed. And hell, he wasn't short on looks either. Tall, blonde and muscular, charisma on legs. He could chat up the girls with a single wink, they were queuing up to date our Gaz.

"So where you heading, Lou?" he enquired. "Looks like a mean machine….got a chick in tow?"

At that moment Ellie emerged, teasing a loose curl into line as she took in the suave stranger paused by the bike.

"Just the kid sister, I'm afraid."

Acutely aware that time was passing rapidly he cast her a glance.

"Ell, get a move on. Need to call in at Tesco I promised Kale I'd fetch some burgers and….."

"Woah!!" Quilon cut him short. "Think Al a Carte, Cordon Bleu, Free Range….still a lot to learn man."

Quilon was making for the back yard. He sprinted over the makeshift fence and disappeared from view, with Lou wondering what on earth he was up to. Ellie looked at her brother questioningly, the pair of them holding their breath, ears strained for any slight noise or movement that might give them a clue.

In seconds he was back, wielding a large, bulging canvas bag tied haphazardly at the top with a loose knot. As he came closer Lou had the distinct impression that to hang around would not be a good option. Eyes gleaming, mischievously Quilon leapt over the oil shimmering puddles, cradling the squirming sack in his arms. A shrill screeching sound emanated from the palpitating parcel as he flicked the remote to open the Mazda's rear door, slinging the suspicious shipment inside.

"Scram!" he yelled, indicating the bike. "Things could just turn a little 'fowl'."

CHAPTER 2. Lou's Story – 2014

That weird musty smell was the first indication of the nature of their accommodation, hitting Lou's nostrils even before he'd reached the precarious porch. Squeezed sardine like between the old chemist shop and an antiques emporium the house at first appeared derelict, its grimy windows in need of a wash and the crumbling frames a lick of paint. To say it was neglected was an understatement and no one in their right mind would look twice at the crumpled flyer tacked to the gate offering "Vacancies."

Now he wavered again, a shiver running down his spine, as he noted the demonic skull and cross bones that served as a door knocker.

However, the ultimate disappointment came as Lou entered the ten by twelve space Kalen called a bedroom. It housed two iron bedsteads, a set of drawers and an original Victorian fireplace nestled in the chimney breast, its grate empty and unwelcoming. In the window recess was a chair with its back rest missing and hanging cobweb like at the window, a pair of crude curtains. The cracked antique mirror on the far wall only served to reinforce his sense of bad luck.

Ellie had managed to settle herself in at the rear of the building, sharing the south facing room with Perdy and the only one that had en-suite. With the same meagre furniture but the comparative luxury of a portable electric fire. Here Midnight had taken up her usual position on Ellie's duvet purring softly as Lou peered in.

It was of course warmer than his own room, slightly larger, containing two double beds. The décor was a little quaint Lou thought, lilac brocade curtains, matching chenille rugs and above the divan a rather unnerving print of a young girl floating downstream in a river, fully clothed, wistfully gazing up at the sky. The figure had an almost saintly quality, a bizarre subject Lou thought and he felt his stomach lurch. He certainly wouldn't swap it for his cracked mirror.

Lou returned to the corridor and followed Kalen out back to the yard. He'd managed to find a cover for the bike but the sidecar was open to the elements. Immediately to the left of the back door was a hatch way which Kalen opened revealing a ramp leading directly into the cellar. As it happened the converted coffin, though incredibly cumbersome and unwieldy due to the weight of the new chassis seemed to glide easily down the slope, to rest at peace in the subterranean surroundings.

On entering it was clear that this was indeed a storeroom of some kind. It was dark and gloomy and from the threshold he could just make out some lengths of timber on canvas sheets and a number of shelves with an array of tools. As Kalen struck a match it dawned on Lou then that actually this had been the casket's former home, a funeral parlour of distinction providing a respectful and sensitive service to the bereaved families of Whitby.

This revelation thought Lou, was hardly comforting. Furthermore, the prospect of sleeping directly above this veritable basecamp for the inevitable final journey was decidedly disturbing.

Lou couldn't wait to make his excuses and return to his room. Grim as it was the sparsely furnished sleeping quarters were somehow more appealing. As he made his way upstairs he began wondering just how long he could endure the damp and discomfort. He reflected on the dormitories of the Seafarer's Mission, where the homeless gathered, even they he supposed, would offer more respectable lodgings.

Hesitating on the threshold he was aware the door had been opened, maybe to afford the room a much needed breath of fresh air. Lou had difficulty focussing, but by the far window he could vaguely make out a hunched figure. There was a distinctly nauseating smell of mothballs that he'd not noticed before and a strange hollow pulsing sound which he assumed was a tap dripping somewhere. A small fire crackled and hissed in the ebony grate sending a puff of grey smoke, silently swirling around the iron bed frames like an incoming fog.

It was his first meeting with Dag, a steam punk from Glasgow. He hadn't been part of the original group down at the studios. His eyes were friendly enough, clear and honey coloured but his voice was deep and throaty like treacle, his rich accent incongruous and acutely at odds with the local seaport spiel.

"Ochs! Man," said the Glaswegian. "You must be Lou."

There was a distant look in his eyes, as though he were staring straight through you and it was at this point Lou began to wonder just how long he could endure this.

What exactly was he thinking of anyway? He wasn't one of them, not a Goth or a Punk. So why was he here?

The place was depressing, deathly cold and no one with any sense would want to lodge here, in this God forsaken hovel. Still, they'd only just arrived.

Besides there was the promise of a Barbeque this evening, a welcome party of sorts. Lou's presence was expected.... no demanded and to refuse was not an option. The mere thought of a scene with his formidable friend, Kalen was more than enough to persuade him to stay. At least for the time being.

Kalen took the lead, striding ahead through the winding streets, past dimly lit shops and the sleepy, shuttered cafes his studded boots chiming rhythmically on the cobbles in tune with the familiar whistle. He moved swiftly, slipping by passages, jumping the iron grates and side tracking the shop hoardings that lined the narrow pavements.

Like the Pied Piper, he demanded a following. Curious children stopped spellbound, shopkeepers stared and a calculating cat dodged his determined footfall. Snaking the alleyways unperturbed, his matted locks flowing serpent-like from beneath the three cornered hat. His mind on the pleasures of the forthcoming evening with never a doubt his partisans were in pursuit.

Lou stood in the doorway, adjusting his collar he called to the others. The chill of the evening met his nostrils as he waited clutching the four pack and fumbling in his pocket for his mobile.

Where was his sister? She'd made herself scarce since their arrival. It happened every time. Elusive Ellie they called her.

Why was it always up to him to babysit, watch over her, tamper with her texts, look over her lovers, pacify and protect her?

“Ell” he called.

The feeble tones echoed through the hollow interior. He was more than a little irritated. It was bad enough supervising her on home ground but here in an alien environment, the glitz of the shop windows, the narrow streets teaming with strangers.....and they didn't come any stranger, this weekend.

Dag emerged, ignoring the hairy anthropoid sliding surreptitiously down the pallid cheekbone. Bubbling laughter emanated from the passageway as Ellie and the girls followed on, feather boas flying and Perdy in hot pursuit of her idol. She’d taken a shine to Kalen way back, always at his beck and call, running his errands - besotted and bewitched.

Merle emerged clinging on to her hero’s arm like a limpet, her eyes drinking in the muscular shoulders and quickening her step. There was no sign of Quilon. His volunteering duties at the Seafarer’s mission usually kept him busy till the early hours, so no one was in the least surprised.

Lou grabbed Ellie’s hand and they flew like the wind down the Spartan street the winter sunshine on its downward journey, penetrating like a laser beam. Their clandestine commander made no allowances, each and every one of the company would be there, pledging their troth, smoking the pipe, all for one and one for all.

As the sun began to set in the west they mounted the sandstone steps, one hundred and ninety nine in all, a damp air drifting in from the sea, the scream of the gulls filling their senses. At the summit the sun lay spent in the west, weary from its day's journey.

Assembled by the gate they entered the allotment that bordered the graveyard. Kalen was already there poised by the brazier shifting the metal grid to ignite the strands of straw and kindle they'd managed to collect from the undergrowth, his hands working deftly with the brittle sticks. Surprisingly, Quilon emerged from the shadows, the magician's assistant, and a welcome ally.

"Here let me," he offered.

He was often absent from social events and since he'd been abroad for some months he had been down to re-register as a volunteer to continue his charity work at the Seafarer's Mission.

Within seconds he was engulfed, a pat on the back, a kiss on the cheek; a rekindling of old friendships. His lack of punctuality overlooked, he was generally respected for the valuable support he offered to the less fortunate.

Aware of the switch in focus, Kalen stepped forward. The show of enthusiasm from the rest of the group was decidedly slow and he gestured to the branches strewn at the base of hedgerow.

"Get too it," he yelled, tone crisp and compelling.

Before long the bonfire was lit and everyone stretched out on blankets.

In the warm glow, shadows danced leaping higher as the hum of conversation filled the air. Their appetites whetted by the spit of spicy sausage and the unwinding effect brought on by the lager.

Quilon didn't waste a second. Reaching into the sack he brought out his poultry offering that had been residing in the makeshift pen in the backyard. As the bag was opened a cheer went up, followed by a complimentary applause. Unfortunately, the squawking bird was becoming more of a nuisance than an asset now. Shaking the scraggy throat, he mumbled incantations as he fought to keep it still. Howls of laughter came from the onlookers who advanced in a bid to contain the chicken, their promise of a robust meal quickly disappearing.

"Hold it right there, Lou," said Hathus.

Grab it. Don't let it get away ....whoa, whoa."

Squawking and kicking out, desperate for freedom it broke free.

“Hey,” said Lou. “After it!”

But the bird was in no mood to linger, somewhat bruised and bewildered it hit the ground and made for the undergrowth. By now the whole company was on their knees searching the surrounding shrubbery while Kalen watched on.

“Enough.....” he shouted, clapping imperially. “Let the entertainment begin.......”

Summoned by their chief the crew gathered ceremoniously around the blazing bonfire, excitedly expectant. Shadows grew as the flames danced higher. Faces aglow with anticipation and tiny stars dotting the sky overhead. Lou took to the groundsheet next to Kalen his boots discarded. He made a mental note of Ellie's whereabouts. He had after all promised to look out for her. She and Merle had retreated to the yew tree in the graveyard, oblivious to the macho gathering and for the moment at least she was safe and sound, free from male attention yet close enough for Lou to keep his vigil.

There was a lull in the conversations as heads pivoted to greet a faint but captivating sound. From the direction of the abbey came a doleful melody floating in the night air. But there was no sign of the singer. Lou put down his lager and peered into the gloom a strange feeling stirring inside him, and his temperature rising, un-seasonally. He glanced momentarily toward the churchyard gate and reassured by his sister's familiar laughter he returned immediately to more interesting events.

Kalen had concealed in his tunic an ancient flagon from which he took a draft and passed around the company. It was a strange liquor, sweet, nectar like even, which Lou had difficulty identifying.

The flagon having journeyed full circle was returned and Lou took another mouthful, wiping his lips he scanned the field perimeter in search of the singer. It wasn’t long before she came into view, a distant nymph, illuminated by the rising moon, like a Banshee in the night. She drew closer, the haunting melody increasing in tempo the strangely compelling lyrics lingering on the air. She traced her way round the curve of the trees, caressing the leafy branches and swaying with the rhythm.

The advancing figure became the primary focus of the group as she danced bold and barefoot to centre stage, the folds of her translucent gown fluttering in the sea breeze. Lou's jaw dropped as she swayed, tantalisingly beside the fire, a seductive smile playing easily across the full lips, the hypnotic eyes and curious chant casting a strange spell. Kalan nudged him in the ribs, terminating his trance and reviving the present.

“She's a stunner isn't she Lou?” he said.

The totally unexpected vision had rendered him speechless, his pupils firmly embedded in the advancing cleavage, the manicured hands floating before him, aided by the persistent rhythm they seemed to take control, enticing, beckoning. She sang in a strange tongue, runic phrases with an impelling melody. Then he realised she was making a play for him.

Lou couldn't remember the last time he had been aroused like this, certainly not "since Suzy" and maybe he'd never felt like this before. There was a stirring in his loins, an overwhelming desire to leap up and devour her....but he remained there mesmerised, the ceremony continuing. He suddenly felt quite uplifted, euphoric even, wallowing in the effects of the strange liquor. He was suddenly helpless, his legs numb his body paralysed, controlled by an outside force.

As the music swelled, the tempo increased again and a distant drumming spurred the onlookers who began chanting in monotonous chorus. The sting of wood smoke mixed with the weed and the dubious drink caused him to sway involuntarily. As he watched captivated, the siren pressed on with her seduction. Lou was transfixed and he couldn't tear his eyes from her.

"Who is she?"

But Kalen's answer was lost in the musical frenzy as the temptress touched the higher notes and edged a little closer to the flames. Her loose garment ruffled by the wind she danced within inches of the bonfire.

Lou flinched. "Isn't that just a little risky?"

"Relax, Lou.....maybe it's time to live a little dangerously"

Kalen shrunk back into the shadows as the singer advanced again, her limped form hovering within inches of his sweat beaded brow.

Wait.....his conscience called. Wait.... didn't you promise? But the moment had gone and although his eyes flickered momentarily in Eleanor's direction the magic was much stronger. It was in fact overwhelming and he rose slowly, willingly. Lured by the hypnotic eyes he glided across the open ground skirting the fire as she beckoned him closer. In seconds he was locked in her arms, their bodies converging, obeying her every command. Back and forth in the shadows, the music in crescendo, their faces illuminated - startlingly surreal in the fanning flames. The sorceress had stolen his soul and now there was no going back.

The company watched as the couple departed, hand in hand, squeezing through the bramble hedge and into the woodland beyond.

Lou had never experienced torture of course, but he assumed it couldn't be any worse than this. There was a demon drum thumping in his head and the inside of his mouth tasted like a navvies armpit. The iron bedstead groaned beneath him sending a sharp twinge down his back and there was a nausea lurking deep in his stomach. He opened his eyes, turning his head toward the window in an effort to determine the time.

The sun was pretty high, streaking unmercifully through the cobweb curtains. With significant effort he managed to roll over, sitting upright he peered through bloodshot eyes at the reflection in the broken glass. There was no other sound above the pounding of his head and he assumed he was alone. In the dim light he was just able to make out the congealing blood at his temples, the angry bruise on his cheek and the vicious scratches that covered his forehead and arms.

The unfamiliar face in the mirror stared at him, not one head but two and the room was spinning. He frowned back, at a loss to know just how long he'd lain there or how in fact he'd made his return. The previous night, the aftermath of the Barbeque was a complete blank, a total mystery, an empty page.

Lou strained his ears. There was definitely no-one about. No wood burning in the fire, no sound of dripping taps and no hint of mothballs. The room was empty, the other bed vacant with just a few cans in military precision on the mantelpiece.

He shuddered involuntarily drawing back the skimpy coverlet, his eyes suddenly wide as he discovered he was stark naked beneath the bedclothes. Clothes folded meticulously on the broken chair, his mobile connected, charging on the top. Tidy was not a word he registered with so whoever had accompanied him back last night......had not only undressed him but carried out all the necessary housekeeping duties. He thought briefly of Ellie and then drew a line under that; her bedroom at home was like a veritable jumble sale.

Oh God, Ellie. Where was she? Now he was fully awake.

If he hadn't been so preoccupied, so easily persuaded last night, so utterly wrecked this would never have happened.

His head still pounding he threw back the covers and snatched at his underwear. It was cold and clammy and his boxers were decidedly damp. The silence in the house was unreal and as he hovered by the window pulling on his shirt he realised his hunch had been right. It was way after noon.

The corridor was even colder without socks, which were strangely absent and his shoes were nowhere to be seen either. He checked the girl's room, it was empty, even the silken duvet where Midnight usually lay appeared unruffled, the only signs of life were in the kitchen. The lingering toast smell and a sink full of crockery.

He'd been so sure they'd all be still sleeping but there was an uneasiness at the back of his mind that grew by the second.

In the front porch now he was surprised to see his jacket hung squarely on the peg nearest the door and his footwear perfectly polished and stationed on a shoe tree, together with his socks… ready to walk, as if displayed in a shop window.

Lou slipped them on, adjusted his collar, wincing as he opened the creaking door. He listened once more desperate for a sign that at least one of the tenants might be home. The grandfather clock chimed, hitting the remaining raw nerve in his head and ending his confusion. Thunder in triplicate, it reverberated through the corridor. Three in the afternoon and he'd managed to sleep the clock round.

It was of course October and the weather was inclement, showers and a biting wind, a stark contrast to the evening before. He walked swiftly, mindful of the maze of unfamiliar streets, the concealed alleyways, the seedy bars.

He just needed to make sure Ellie was safe. He'd ride out the scathing comments, smutty remarks from the others until he could piece together the events of last night but for now his only concern was for his sister. He took the winding street toward the hundred and ninety nine steps, noting the empty walkways devoid of day trippers and holiday makers, harbouring only the odd shop keeper, dressing windows or locking up for the night.

The White Horse and Griffin was all in darkness, tables folded neatly in the back courtyard, too early for the drinkers- the only clients a pair of scavenging seagulls. Lou wasted no time, if they weren't in the pub then maybe they'd be trawling the late night boutiques, the twenty four hour coffee shops, queuing for fish and chips. But, never the less he was drawn to the bay. The sound and scent of the ocean was always a magnate for Ellie, plastered in Ambre Solar, a hat and sunglasses to avoid the harmful rays she'd always loved to be at the beach.

In the west the sun was descending quickly now, leaving a rosy glow above the line of terracotta roofs, their chimneys alive with swirls of grey smoke as he hurried through the square and down between the stone cottages. Emerging from the tight alleyway he reached the strip that was Tate Hill sands, the seaweed spray keen in his nostrils. He stopped, cursing the hangover and wishing he'd never laid eyes on Whitby.

He didn't bother to remove his shoes as he stepped onto the wet sand. It was dropping dark, little rain clouds darting wildly in the skies above his head as the breakers crashed onto the shore and retreated again. Lou had also loved the seaside as a child, Aunt May would bring them for several days at a time in the holidays, to paddle in the shallows, build sand castles, guzzle dripping ice lollies. Such a treat, a lasting memory but tinged always with the sadness of their parents absence and the realisation that their childhood would always be like that.

Suddenly there was a warm breeze, quite strange for late October, Lou thought. It caused him to pause and look about him. There was no one around but laying idly on the sand was an abandoned bucket and spade, a splintered toy sailing ship and some paper flags fluttering in a collapsed castle. Lou bent down, intrigued to see the emblems, his past life momentarily flashing past. As he lifted it a gust of wind wafted the little flag high in the air. It fluttered there for a moment then flew over in the direction of the rocks. He remembered the tiny limpet pools he and Ellie had discovered there so long ago and he stared longingly at the rugged outcrop wishing he could be cast back in time, innocent and free enjoying a natural, average family holiday.

Lou blinked. He thought he'd been alone on the stretch of sand, a solitary beach comber enjoying the privacy of a secluded shore but if he wasn't mistaken somewhere out there on the farthest crop was a figure. Lou didn't trust himself of course his perceptions weren't that clear at present, blurred images, double vision and that swimming feeling alongside the thumping in his head. He stared hard.

Above the swirling waters of the North Sea, cross legged on the farthest rock Lou was sure he could see a mermaid. He blinked, trying to focus. Long platinum locks falling in ringlets, she sat with her back to him, a strange melody floating across the sand, punctuated only by the sound of a melodious voice. A siren?

Closing his eyes firmly he shook his head vigorously. Hallucinating again, he thought. Curse Kalen and his obnoxious potions.

At that moment the spell was broken and as he stumbled forward the girl stopped playing and turned.

"Hi!" she smiled, bright and radiant a perfect contrast to the wintery landscape.

"Sorry did I startle you?"

Lou began wishing again but this time his yearning was for the present. Whatever the past held suddenly the future look instantly brighter.

"No," he shouted, above the waves and the raucous birds wheeling above them. "I'm sure it was me that disturbed you."

The very sight of her made Lou melt inside, his hangover all but evaporating together with the recent longings for home. She stood to introduce herself, holding out a small white hand in greeting.

"I'm Nette," she said.

"Lou.... Lou Bannister."

He shook her hand firmly a little self-conscious, aware of his bleary eyes and pale complexion. Then he looked over her shoulder, scanning the rock beyond.

"I come down here to practice sometimes," she gestured to the abandoned guitar. "It's quiet and the sea is so beautiful at this time of day."

Turning she retrieved the instrument then stepped back down beside him.

For a brief second their eyes met. They twinkled in the fading light and an amused smile flickered across her face as though she'd read his mind.

"Not seen any lately," she mused. "But the sailors' will tell you of sightings on moonlit nights."

Lou blushed, feeling suddenly idiotic.

They headed back along the beach, the tide rippling close to their feet and the light fading fast. Lou felt the dreaded nausea again and the wild panic returning.

"I'm looking for my sister," he blurted." Have you seen anyone? Tall, blonde around sixteen?"

The mistaken mermaid shook her head slowly, "You're not from round here are you?"

"Well, no Pudsey actually. I'm not sure how long Ellie's been gone or even who she's with."

As they neared the little patch of sand where the flags had been Lou noticed two distinct sets of small footprints, aside from his own. They were leading to the rocks that bordered the far side of the bay, an ideal playground for youngsters but easily a danger with the incoming tide. Lou recalled a lucky escape at Cleethorpes, with Aunt May, when they'd been caught in the breakers; he and Ellie marooned on a rocky ledge.

They stood anticipating the sound of childish voices, returning to collect their playthings before the sun set or the tide caught them out. But there wasn't a sound.

"No, I didn't see anyone," she said as they scanned the line of the land, expecting at any moment to clap eyes on the youngsters.

"Hope they got home safely it's getting late and the tides turning fast."

Nette traced the flooded imprints with the tip of her toe.

“And your sister…you think she came this way?”

Lou hesitated, then shrugged.

”I’m heading back through the town, I’ll walk with you if want and we can check in all the tourist spots on the way,” she said.

Lou registered her sincerity, the flash of concern as she noted the grazing to his face and the urgency in his voice. He felt a connection between them as though the shaking of hands had linked them in some strange and surreal way; like an electrical circuit, creating the vital spark.

He walked beside her, quickening his step to keep up as she darted here and there through dark passageways, and up hidden stairways making the most of the newly lit streets and the glowing interiors of the town’s taverns. As Nette guided him to the most popular attractions Lou talked. He told her about Ellie, her personality, her irritating little habits, the pathetic specimen of a boyfriend and the never ending duty of care for his wayward sister.

His companion chatted back, asking questions, offering brief words of reassurance as she ran, taking his hand to lead him along unfamiliar paths, and bobbing under weathered arches before finally arriving in the main shopping street. Aside from the welcome glow of the lamps the only glimmer of light they could see now was from the Local Newsagents where Nette stopped and turned.

“Just nip in for my order Lou, I won’t be a sec.”

In an instant she had slipped through the tiny doorway, like Alice in Wonderland, a mythical figure stepping out of his dream. Lou lent breathlessly against the lamp post desperately hoping his fantasy would return. It was then that he saw the headline on the advertising board. The white sheet glaring at him, the erratic print emphasising the horror of the situation.

“PUDSEY TEENAGER MISSING IN WHITBY…..SEARCH AREA WIDENED! “

Lou went cold, his hands trembled and when Nette returned he was routed to the spot.

“Oh my God…” he was saying. “I knew something was wrong, that’s where they are….they’re all out looking.”

The Evening News slipped from beneath Nette’s arm as they stood side by side, staring at the billboard. She shook her head, the reassurance she’d given him earlier seeming oddly futile now. He felt her arm around his shoulder, the hand that squeezed his to stop it from shaking. All he could do was stare at the headline in disbelief.

"No Lou, don't think like that.....it'll be Ok you'll see."

CHAPTER 3. Kate's story – 1914

Newly painted railings, silver and green sped past on the promenade, the wooden benches and side stalls flashed nearby as gulls flew overhead. The shoes felt tight, her heart fit to burst but Kate didn't slow down at all. Reaching the bluff beach steps she hesitated but only for a second before sprinting down toward to the beach, discarding the ill-fitting footwear she ignored the warning calls from behind and made a bid for freedom.

The sand between her toes was heavenly, the soothing sea sounds enticing and the only thing that held her back was the threat of the incoming tide. They'd left it a little late this afternoon, the weak winter sunshine giving way to a mass of unruly cloud, hanging menacing above the bay. Kate pulled her wool coat closer, the double breasted front a welcome barrier against the hostile North Sea. Her voice faltered as she called over her shoulder.

"It 'snot safe, Kate." said the young boy, in pursuit.

"Don't dawdle....tides coming in," she replied taking the numb little hand in hers.

As the sun sank even lower on the horizon, the tide sweeping closer they neared the familiar rock cluster emerging from the sea spray where earlier they'd created sand castles. They'd been warned then about the debris on the beach, cotton wool, splintered crutches, and worst of all, syringes. A mounting memorial to the recent disaster that had devastated the East Coast community.

But Kate was becoming that indomitable, intrepid adventurer and would stop at nothing to reach her goal. Edward was familiar with his cousin's tenacity and knew better than to quibble, besides time was of the essence, his sodden feet a startling caution.

Here they mounted the boulders with care, the slippery surface delaying them as they spread their toes to get a grip. Edward floundered like an eel, catching his ankle in a barnacled fissure and yelling out briefly. Kate turned to free him, then they continued unperturbed.

At the mouth of the cave a chill air brought them to a standstill, taking their breath away momentarily. With eyes wide and hands lingering on the clammy boulders obscuring the opening, their fingers felt numb. Neither spoke as they listened, to the waves crashing, the wind whining and a very small voice from within.

Instantly Kate was through the small gap feeling her way along the restricting walkway, following the muted sound, beckoning and compelling. Edward followed his heart thumping. He wished he were back home in the drawing room, listening to the family gossip, the spit of the logs on the fire and waiting for his sheets to be turned down. He clutched the hem of Kate's coat nervously as they became aware of a faint glimmer of light around the corner and a feeble sound.

"Who goes there?"

Huddled together, crouched in the confines of the inner cavern, they froze.

The little light they had been attracted to, emanated from a small fire not a foot from where they stood. Edward released his grip on Kate's coat tails, attempting a break for the beach but his cousin was quick to stall him. Fearlessly she peered into the cavern, challenging the gloom her eyes focussed on the sandy floor.

Beyond the prancing flames lay a half- naked man draped in a seaweed coverlet. It was difficult to make out the features in the darkness and although his lips appeared dry and sore, his eyes held a certain hopeful gleam. His face was taut like a bronze mask, streaked with silt from the cave walls. Beside him was a battered leather knapsack, a water bottle and a bundle of damp twigs.

"Who goes there?" the voice demanded again.

Now the fear seemed gone from Kate at the sight of a mere mortal and she advanced boldly, her mind relieved of smugglers and sea monsters.

"It's I.....Kate Pickering. I knew you were here......I knew you were alive."

The voice became a man before their eyes. The face racked with pain, the features contorted and strangely oscillating in the feeble flames, he managed to raise himself to half-mast before responding.

"Kate Pickering, eh?" he said." And you knew I was here?

By now the intrepid two had emerged fully into the stranger's domain the glow from the little fire illuminating their faces. Edward shuddered anxiously, inspecting the bleak surroundings, with less faith in their new acquaintance than his cousin.

"Who are you?" Kate dared.

The stranger staring back seemed amused, a flicker of a smile tickled around his lips, the muddy cheeks lifting momentarily before he winced with discomfort. Recovering instantly he reached out for his leg concealed beneath the seaweed coverlet, grimacing again. Kate was quick to respond.

"You're injured...." she said.

"Don't take heed of me, young miss," he warned. "The tides on the turn, you shouldn't delay."

He was right, of course. The thunder of the breakers was increasing now, the sun would soon be gone. Kate turned reluctant to leave but mindful of the elements she took Edwards trembling hand in hers and returned to the small opening. She glanced at the few twigs, the water bottle that was all but empty and she knew the mysterious cave dweller to be in the utmost danger.

"I'll be back.... please don't alarm yourself. I'll get help."

Without a backward glance they were retracing their steps in the virtual darkness, lungs hungry for air their feet cold and clammy. Without further hesitation they made for the beach locating a boulder. And with only seconds to spare they secured the entrance. They knew if they stayed a moment longer the sea would take them.

At the age of twelve young Katherine Pickering was sharp as a dagger, transparent as glass and remarkably resolute for her years. She also had a heart of gold which shone unashamedly through the hazel eyes with a growing intensity. In fact Kate could not stand injustice and recently she had begun to develop a curious yet remarkable intuition, which presently was on high since the arrival of their new governess, Maria Hicks. Kate could sense the woman's malevolence in every part of her being, from the crest of her silken head to the very tip of her toes. She touched the nerve endings, gathered her goose bumps, tarnishing her every dream.

The thin, irate face flushed with running leaned over the railing, the auburn hair once coiled neatly in a bun at the nape of her neck floated free. She shouted, shaking her fists wildly and looking for all the world Kate though, like a manic Methuselah.

"Hold it right there, young lady," Hicks hollered, as they reached the top step and sped past her along the promenade.

Edward halted obediently when summoned, tied his dangling laces and straightened his collar but Kate wasn't to be deterred. Following the familiar route home, heart racing she stumbled through the gate, crossing the drive, then mounting the steps two at a time. This was an emergency, a matter of life and death and there was only one person who could save the day. That person was her father.

"Papa," she shouted. "Papa, come quickly."

To her dismay the mahogany door glided open revealing an unexpected shower of people, taking tea and cake in the Pickering's comfortable drawing room. Kate blushed, she would never have entered had she known they had guests and stood speechless in the aperture.

The moment of silence that followed was brief as her father appeared from the throng, peering thoughtfully at her through his monocle.

"Oh Kate, how lovely ....come and join us," he beckoned.

It was not what Kate had expected when she came to tell her news and quickly she apologised and retreated, closing the door silently behind her.

Whatever would she do now? Her father was the most conscientious and caring person in the world, and only he could help. Yet, there was no time to lose or she would not be able to guarantee the stranger would survive the night.

Who else could she turn to? Charles Henry Pickering notable and respected by the whole of Whitby and beyond for his charitable work and business standing. Only he could save the day.

Kate had barely taken a step across the hall when the Drawing Room door opened, revealing the man himself.

"Well, my little sunshine, whatever is the matter?"

Kate had a way of manoeuvring her father, altering his course of events, bending decisions. It was the look she gave him, the sincerity in her eyes; that tone of voice and more recently the dogged determination to stand up for her beliefs. He bent down holding her at arm's length, to measure the concern on her face and he asked again.

Her response was slow, mindful of the company awaiting his return but once he'd heard the story she was absolutely sure, without the shred of a doubt, that she could rely on his wholehearted support.

The current hustle and bustle in the Pickering household was nothing unusual but since the arrival of the handsome stranger, Number 32 had started to resemble an overbooked guesthouse. It had only been a couple of days since the hospital ship, Rohilla had gone aground in the bay, a shocking tragedy and such great loss of human life Not to mention the futile waste of medical equipment and resources that had been destined for Dunkirk.

The community had been swift to respond with many of the local families offering temporary accommodation to survivors and true to form Charles Pickering, had been first in line to open his doors. So, with not a hand to spare, or a room vacant everyone had to pull their weight.

Kate lingered on the back stairs watching the activity. She loved the lively chatter and the waft of freshly laundered linen that emanated from the kitchen in the early morning and later in the day the heavenly aroma of Mrs Andrew's home cooking.

Mrs. Dawson, not easily ruffled wiped her hands on the starched apron and shook her head.

"Whatever next, I ask myself," said the weary housekeeper.

The gaslights were lit in the downstairs kitchen now as the staff gathered to air their grievances. Dorothy laid the table with four places mindful of cook's rantings and desperate to avoid any extra duties. She'd spent the previous evening preparing the spare bedroom at very short notice for the latest visitor and she sincerely hoped she could retire this evening before midnight.

"I really don't know," Mrs Dawson continued. "What with Master Edward arriving last week and Mrs Anna due at any moment we'll shortly be running out of clean bed linen."

Mr.Grigg entered adjusting his neatly folded cravat with a frown. It was his nightly duty to run the security checks, sliding the bolts on the outer doors and making sure their limited staff were all safely within and available if called upon. It was also his undertaking as butler, to prepare the rotas for the coming week and that was his intention this evening.

"They need more blankets at once for Mr.er....the new gentleman upstairs, Dorothy. Can you see to that?" he said.

"Well, snap too it young lady and whilst your about it lay the fire in the south wing guest room ready for Mrs Anna," he added.

Mrs. Andrews was a competent cook, always ready to try new recipes, rich delicacies from Switzerland and France, traditional Scottish dishes and the exceptional local seafood. Recently of course, due to the war restrictions her dishes had been less extravagant despite her admirable culinary skills.

Mr.Grigg hovered by the stove. "Mrs Pickering has requested that the gentleman should have fresh cow's milk with his porridge every morning a lightly boiled egg and fresh fruit. Apparently it's vital for his swift recovery," he instructed.

Kate watched the housemaid scurrying round the kitchen. She retrieved a pile of bedlinen from the worktop and squeezed past the beady eyed butler making her way toward the back stairs. It was darker in the corridors, stone cold underfoot with damp patches reaching out from the ceilings, as Kate trailed her. Dorothy shivered. She was running late again, her arms weak with carrying wood for the fires and her knees so sore from the constant scrubbing.

In the upstairs lobby lay a scattering of wet clothes, a bedraggled kite with the string missing and a bucket and spade. Dorothy's eyes widened and she sighed. Things just weren't the same around here lately she had to admit. Due to the recent disaster, routines had changed and duties had doubled with the household had taking on a rather a different role.

Esther emerged from the drawing room dressed for dinner, her cheeks flushed she halted by the vestibule feeling the drift of cool air from the doorway.

“Ah, Dorothy, there you are. Could you advise Mrs Dawson that our gentleman friend will be taking a light supper in his room tonight?”

“Yes Ma’am.”

In the evening glow Mrs Pickering looked stunning, her coiffured hair, the elegant gown, the cluster of diamonds at her neck, as befitting the lady of the house. In the past few days Kate’s admiration for her mother had escalated Apart from numerous charities she supported, the exceptional care and support she gave her staff, she'd never thought twice about opening up her home to survivors of the storm.

Now she nodded dismissively at Dorothy, smiling as she swept gracefully through the hallway and into the dining room. Her head was full of the supper menus she'd discussed with her housekeeper today and eyes shone confidently, secure in the knowledge that everything was in hand.

“It must be so strange to know so little about who you are,” Charles was thinking out loud.

Her husband had taken up his usual stance, hands on hips in the familiar smoking jacket, his eyes twinkling in the firelights glow. Kate watched from the doorway eager for any further news on the mysterious stranger.

“To not even be aware of your name, your home ….your family, well it's the least we can do Esther in this time of crisis and Lawrence has said he’ll call in between surgeries.”

Charles had great faith in his brother in law as a doctor but the recent disaster had meant that beside his daily surgery Dr Hinton was also helping out with survivors at the local hospital.

It was warm by the fireside but Charles was restless, he felt somehow responsible for the stranger in his household, the tension mounting on his face. He reached and rang downstairs, then joined his wife at the table. He planted a kiss on her cheek, still deep in thought his salt grey head nodding thoughtfully as he pondered on the events of the day.

The drapes drawn, the candelabra lit, they awaited the evening meal.

"Did he have anything with him, Charles?" Esther enquired.

Her husband took a deep breath, adjusted his cravat and shook his head.

"Nothing to identify him at all?"

"Just a leather flask and an empty bottle containing an old photograph, apparently."

Mrs Pickering turned, anticipating the arrival of supper as the children's excitable laughter filtered through the dining room.

"He's awake...he's awake," Kate informed them. "Can we go up now?"

The children's father looked over disapprovingly at his young daughter and nephew as they entered. Raising his eyebrows he beckoned to them. It was late, the nursery was calling and dinner was about to be served.

"Please, please Pa," she pleaded. "You promised, you promised."

It wasn't in Kate's nature to back down and looking into the deep and pleading Pickering eyes he realised it was a lost cause. Esther smiled wearily. She knew her daughter to be both plucky and determined. It was a foregone conclusion, Charles would of course give in.

"Hicks can accompany you and mind you only stay a few minutes...the man is still very poorly and needs to rest."

Her father took the small hand in his, squeezed it fondly and glanced over at his nephew. Edward had little to say for himself, a relative newcomer and unfamiliar with the routines of the household he stepped forward tentatively.

"What's his name the mister?"

"Well, we're not too sure young Edward, he's had a nasty bump to the head and Dr Hinton says he's suffering from some kind of shock."

"How awful. He must have a name though....."

"He's a mystery, Edward," Kate said. "Let's go ask him."

Esther rose to escort them to the door, cautioning them she summoned the governess.

"Don't pester the man though, dears. As your father said, Kate, he's still extremely ill."

In the hallway Hicks was waiting, the staunch features putting an end to their frivolity, though nothing could dampen their enthusiasm. She led them ceremoniously through the hallway military fashion, her grey flannel skirt silently dusting the floor, a heavy bunch of keys bumping rhythmically at her thigh, in tune with their steps.

Along the first floor landing, past the master bedroom, then beyond to the rear of the house. Here they mounted a further set of stairs, little used but with the handrails recently dusted. As they reached the next landing Kate noted the open widows and the fresh smell of lavender.

Hicks continued to the very end of the corridor, to a room Kate had rarely visited that was kept for special guests. It was one of the few that had an adjoined bathroom, which like the others with additional facilities had been restored to their former glory. Since the shipwreck, the house had seen a constant flurry of visitors, VAD nurses, GP's and patients with a varying degree of need. This was where they came to recuperate, rest and hopefully in the very near future return to their own families.

It was quiet and Hicks stopped at the sick room bending her head to listen. Heavy snoring and they would no doubt turn away, leaving the gentleman to his much needed rest. But, within a second Hicks had rapped on the door and gingerly turned the handle.

Inside the room was airy but bathed in darkness, the heavy drapes shutting out any stray beams from the surrounding streetlights.

The little fire burning in the grate was enough to take off the chill, casting a rosy glow on the cherry wood furnishings and giving the room a welcoming feel.

Kate and Edward stepped inside apprehensively and peered over toward the bed. It was apparent that the patient was sleeping and as their governess adjusted the gas lamps Kate could see the familiar features, calm and serene, his body cocooned in white linen, topped by a silk eiderdown.

"Be mindful of your mother and don't outstay your welcome," Hicks told them. "And leave the lights low he needs to rest."

Sometime passed as Kate began to think he would never wake up but then she saw a flicker of his lashes, a twitch of the pale cheek and finally he opened his eyes.

He groaned, a brief moment of pain crossing his face and his brow furrowed.

"Oh....sorry I didn't know you were there," he said.

Peering at them intrusively, he shifted closer to the edge of the bed, measuring their height and stature with a single glance. He relaxed back into the security of the pillow but continued to reach out with a tremoring hand.

"We didn't mean to disturb you," Kate began.

"How m-m-many are there of you.....I can't see too well."

"Only me and Kate here, we just wanted to check you were alright Mister....Mister...." her cousin continued.

His voice was small and timid, but starkly genuine.

"I'm getting better by the minute, thanks to you and your family." said the man. "But I'm not good company j-j just yet."

The clock on the landing struck seven, which sent a spasm across the man's face again and he turned away pulling the sheet up over his head. Kate tugged at Edward's sleeve and they moved slowly toward the door.

Hicks returned, dimming the lamps and re arranging the bedcovers before turning the logs. It was time to leave. As they reached the threshold Kate paused and took one more look at the mysterious stranger.

"Thank you little Miss," he called. "And you Master Edward.....maybe you could stop by again when I'm better company."

Outside in the corridor, Hicks closed the door quietly and drew them to one side.

"Don't be fooled now," she whispered. "He's not to be trusted and you should be wary, very wary. We don't know who he is and until we do you'll stay away if you have any sense at all."

"What a charming man and what a sad story, Charles." said the pretty but pale faced guest at the Pickering table.

Distinctly elegant in her mourning gown, the doting aunt summoned her, arms outstretched, seeking comfort in the seraphic smile. Anna could sense Kate's keen sense of responsibility for the mystery man's welfare. Replacing the teacup she shook her head, a flicker of anxiety in her keen eye told of compassion, even in the darkest days of her own suffering.

"And he's no recollection at all?"

"None whatsoever, Anna. Apparently his mind is a complete blank."

Charles looked saddened as he related the events of the past few days. The terrible storm, the ship grounded on the Nab and how the whole town came out to help with the rescue operation. As if they hadn't been challenged enough with the onset of the war, the threat of landmines and the dreadful waste of young lives on the front. And then the arrival of the stranger - a mystery man, a vagrant maybe or a survivor of the storm? They had no idea but it was the least they could do in the circumstances, to take him in.

In the quiet of the afternoon a clock chimed bringing the conversation to an abrupt halt. Kate broke the silence, her curiosity surfacing again.

"He looks almost healed to me… when is Dr Hinton coming again, Mama?"

Esther was hesitant, never sure how much information was proper for such a young enquirer. She glanced over at her husband looking for assistance and carefully folded her napkin.

"The physical wounds are healing, sweetie but sometimes the problems are not with the body but within the mind," Charles volunteered.

"I'm not sure what you mean, Papa," Kate persisted. It was all so difficult to take in.

"So he has a part of his brain missing, how did that happen?"

Anna slipped a comforting arm around her niece's shoulder, holding her close.

"What your father means is that we have absolutely no idea who he is. He has no recollection of who he is or where he comes from. For some strange reason, of which we are not certain…… he has completely lost his memory."

"But can't Dr Hinton do anything to help?"

"Well, sweetie he will look in tomorrow but for now it's important that the gentleman rests. And that means no visitors this afternoon," her father added.

Kate's face crumpled. It wasn't the answer she'd been hoping for. She and Edward had planned to call in on the handsome stranger again, really get to know him: ask questions, study the complexity of his face and infiltrate the deepest corners of his mind. Friends, family, survivors of the storm, they always had such interesting lives and so many wonderful tales to tell.

"Well Pa, we won't give up on him. He must remember something, there must be some way we can help."

Charles was always moved by his daughter's sense of responsibility, her obsession with the changing world and her overwhelming desire to protect and preserve. Admiring her dogged determination he proudly recognised it as a Pickering family trait. He smiled down at her.

"We just have to be content that his bones are getting stronger, the cuts and bruises are healing and we shouldn't be too concerned that his name is.........." he stopped, and turned, aware that someone had entered the room.

In the door frame stood Edward, his copper curls fanned by the draft from the hallway, his cherubic face expectant, ready for answers.

"His name is, Pa?" Kate prompted.

"That his name is....... a mystery."

Edward was by his side then. He wasn't the brightest scholar, nor the most mature of seven year olds but he did have the acutest of senses and once he heard something it was firmly lodged in his subconscious, like an anchor aligned to the seabed.

"A...." he said solemnly." Is that 'A' for Albert, Alfred or maybe Angus?"

CHAPTER 4. Kate's story – 1914

And so it was with the help of Edward, that the gentleman acquired a name: Mr. A Mystery. It wasn't the most common of names certainly but everyone who came in contact with the handsome stranger had to agree that it was most appropriate for a person presenting such ongoing intrigue.

The name soon caught on downstairs, to the amusement of the housemaids and even Mr. Grigg was pressured into using the title when anyone came to call. There was of course much speculation as to who he was, where he'd come from and whether he would make a full recovery.

Had he been caught out by the tide? Fallen while walking and hit his head?

Was he just a vagrant residing in the cave?

Or one of the heroic crew of the Rohilla, who'd abandoned ship and made it to the shore, a lucky survivor?

It was at first only family that visited, with Kate and Edward being first in line. They provided winter pansies for his bedside, seasonal fruit and local gossip. Dr Hinton had suggested that making general conversation may trigger his memory and that gradually recollection of past events would return. It would be a slow process though and the patient should not be unduly challenged.

For Kate and Edward though it was a sheer pleasure and a contrast to the tedious hours of study in the schoolroom. Maria Hicks had never been the most inspiring of mentors, keeping strictly to the confines of reading, writing and arithmetic. She had no time for fantasy or fairy tales and strove to engage them in seeking the truth. It was her belief that the only way to educate young minds was to provide an unending array of reference books.

Beside the school room was an anti- room, not exactly a play room because Hicks was not approving of leisure; she deemed it the enterprise of fools. Here they ate their lunch and then made swift excuses.

In the half light of the bedroom, Kate could see that Mr. M was indeed a little livelier this afternoon. He pulled himself up from the pillows and urged them to approach the bed. More handsome too than they had previously imagined him beneath the cuts and bruises as the smile he gave them brought a new light to his eyes they'd never seen before. He had a fine head of mouse brown hair, quite unruly, a tempered face with wide eyes and a tapered chin. And as he turned to greet them Kate could clearly see a raised, dome shaped mole at on the right cheekbone. It was all they could do not to stare.

As they got closer Kate noticed that he was holding something in his hand, a small leather object, which on closer inspection turned out to be the water flask

"I'm so g-glad you came," he said. "It seems like I've lain here for weeks. What day is it, anyway?"

Edward drew closer, putting his hand out toward the stranger in a greeting. He was a little nervous as he remembered his misgivings about the man on that first night down at the cove. But reaching out to return the gesture Edward felt the strength and warmth of his handshake and immediately he was reassured.

"It's Thursday and you've been here five days mister. I've been crossing them off on my calendar and jotting down little notes in my diary," Kate ventured.

For a moment the man didn't speak but his fingers fumbled with the rusty fastener that sealed the flask as he glanced down a puzzled look on the clean cut face.

"I'm not too sure about this," he said. "They tell m-me it was with my belongings."

Edward was curious and leaned over the bed to get a closer view. The container was dented in several places but the seal was still intact.

"Can you pass that knapsack, young man, I b-believe that b-b-belongs to me too."

It was intriguing to watch as he struggled with his injured hands to release the drawstring and it was all the two of them could do to refrain from offering help. But the stranger seemed unperturbed like he was on a mission, seeking a million answers in this vital possession.

He reached inside, tentatively exploring the far corners an expression of hope emerging on the previously blank face. Then with some effort he removed a tarnished gilt frame, amazingly it too was complete and beneath the shattered glass a sepia print; its image of a young women remained startlingly beautiful.

"Can you p-pull the drapes so I can see more easily?" he requested. "The gas lights are not t-t-too helpful at this time of the day."

In the waning afternoon sun Kate could see a vague flicker of recognition in the contours of his face, the furrows of his brow deepened as he tried to make a connection. It was painful to watch him there, his mouth a ridged line, his eyes glazed over, the difficulty he had with speech. And still he struggled, the distress of an empty mind exposed in the deep furrows of his brow. The Pickering empathy was quick to emerge with Kate taking both his hands in hers, as a single tear rolled down his cheek.

Please don't cry," she begged. "We're all here for you....me and Ed, Ma and Pa."

"Yes," her cousin continued. "We can get bandages from the hospital, medicine from the chemist and I know we can find your memory somewhere too, Mr M. It will just take time. Dr Hinton says so and he knows about these things."

As the days grew shorter and the patient grew stronger Kate and Edward visited for longer periods, sometimes well after the lamps had been lit. Mr M always appeared anxious, confused, slurring his words and was regularly halted by a fit of coughing.

Despite the effort Mrs Andrews had put into providing a suitable diet for the patient, he remained pale and thin with little appetite. In the first week he had taken just a little soft fruit, some oatmeal and water. The limited diet, dizzy spells and bruising to his legs keeping him in bed. Yet by the end of the second week he seemed to be making progress and even managed a meal of lightly poached fish.

It became usual for Mr M to relate stories: not true stories for he wasn't one for facts but works of fiction, the absurdities of Edward Lear, the classics of Lewis Carroll and the treasured adventures of Rudyard Kipling. Under the critical eye of their governess they followed the illusive white rabbit, traversed the wildest jungles immersing themselves wholeheartedly in a previously forbidden, fantasy world. His face was animated as he spoke, his voice overflowing with a great warmth. He struggled at times with the words, they rolled around his mouth like a ball bearing in the penny arcade, bouncing off the tongue till they finally made their escape. He had a fascinating timbre, strangely unfamiliar but steeped in sincerity, his voice rising and falling as he told his thrilling tales.

When Mr M became hoarse with the reading, Kate recited poetry and Edward entertained them with his flute playing. It was a strange and impromptu element of his recovery programme which lifted the mood on those chilly winter days, providing a unique therapy which no doubt speeded the patient's recovery.

In fact Dr Hinton had stated that the patient was 'past the worst.' Fortunately the terrible fever he'd suffered on his arrival had eventually subsided and that had been the turning point. Now with his temperature stabilised, his wounds healing they could now work on the restoration of his memory

Aunt Anna was a regular visitor, bringing the morning paper and a brochure of her latest artistic accomplishments. She had recently acquired premises in the square, to be converted into a studio and was currently in the process of promoting her pictures locally. She worked tirelessly to achieve her goal. Mr M was a willing appraiser and he delighted in viewing her work. It seemed his opinion was important to Anna, not only in the subject and quality of her photography and paintings but also with regard to the progress of the new studio.

As the days shortened and Mr M was able to spend afternoons in the drawing room Anna suggested that it was time he walked out. There was a wheelchair in the library and Dr Hinton had already approved a spell in the fresh air. But it was the middle of November and the temperatures were dropping rapidly. The West bay was bitter and for the children the beach was currently off limits.

It was late one afternoon as the clouds began to disperse, Dr Hinton arrived in his Napier. He was concerned about the patient, particularly the extent of his memory loss. Parking up the shiny new automobile he escorted the little group on their usual walk arranging a slight detour to the Cottage Hospital.

Mr M shivered beneath the checked blanket Hicks had placed haphazardly across his knees. He also came under her disapproving gaze - simply tolerated, an addition to her usual duties. Due to the rough cobbles and the reluctant escort it was proving an uncomfortable journey. Kate could see the discomfort etched on his face as he was buffeted through the unfamiliar streets, though he smiled agreeably at their youthful antics. Edward took the lead untangling his kite strings in the strong wind, the collar of his sailor suit flapping round his ears as he raced while Dr Hinton and Anna walked steadily behind them stopping only to give directions.

The ward was large and spotlessly clean with beds in two main aisles, tight rows with a single storage cupboard between. A water jug and glass decorated the cabinets and above each bed was a chart which Kate couldn't quite understand. The whole place was thronging with people and every now and then a patient would scream with pain, reaching out from the blankets in an attempt to attract a nurse's attention. They passed men, women, orderlies and at a number of beds there were doctors tending to patients, mostly males with head injuries, broken limbs and minor abrasions.

It seemed an intrusion, Kate thought. Sleeping patients, overworked nurses battling with the constant stream of visitors who entered the Dettol fresh doors.

Maria Hicks had been distinctly sharp with the children as they left the house, her quiet afternoon now ruined by a sudden change of plan. Kate took in her grim features, the tart voice and stiffness of her starched grey skirts. There was an unnerving undertone to her voice, a hint of cunning which challenged the children daily.

As they neared a side office she hit the foot break with a resounding click, addressing her patient with a synthetic smile as she re arranged the checked blanket. Kate had noticed the way Hicks was constantly adjusting the seat of the wheelchair, fussing over the patient with a consideration she and Edward had never managed to procure.

Dr Hinton tapped lightly on a nearby door.

It was a rosy cheeked, middle aged woman who opened it, her warm welcome pleasant in the strained atmosphere. She nodded to each one of them reassuringly, professionally immaculate in the familiar Red Cross uniform.

"Lawrence, how lovely to see you…I got your message."

Kate had heard the stories of those rescued from the stranded ship, the loss of life and the head injuries, dislocated limbs and many like Mr. M suffering from shock. It was easy to see that the hospitals were filled to capacity and without the support of local townspeople and the voluntary services things could have been far worse. Within minutes Sister Carter had begun her rounds, checking charts, updating notes as she introduced the Pickering family, and their guest at each bedside. Dr Hinton was a regular on the ward and he stopped at intervals, making polite conversation with both staff and patients.

She introduced herself as Sister Helen Carter a volunteer nurse who had been drafted in to help with the growing number of casualties since the disaster and within seconds she was escorting them around the ward.

It was almost dusk as they reached the final bed, a little weary now and all of them eager to depart. They'd seen almost sixty survivors, some sleeping, others just staring into space, a few decidedly alert but not a single glimmer of recognition from any one of them.

"It's difficult Lawrence," Sister Carter said in a whisper. "So much suffering and some of them still no clearer in their minds. Some don't even recognise their own flesh and blood."

She stepped forward, opening the heavy exit door with a contrived smile but suddenly the patient in the bed closest to them sat bolt upright, his eyes afire within his sallow face. Focussing on Mr. M he stared wildly before him and yelling out in a deafening tone, his finger poised menacingly at the incongruous visitor.

"John Jacobson…you blackguard, you rattlesnake. I'd recognise you anywhere, God damn you."

The sounds of the sickbay receded, as the voice reverberated from wall to wall, harsh in the unexpected silence.

"Thought you'd get away with it but you can't hide, you scum of the earth. If I don't take you....... sure the devil will."

Mr. M squirmed, visibly shocked by the outburst. He stared at the apparition in front of him, ridged in his seat, the trembling in his hands suddenly returning. Kate sensed the fear in him, his utter helplessness and noted how the sensitive mouth tightened at the corners. She wanted to run over, fling her arms round the trembling shoulders and hug him, reassure him but she stood her ground. It was Hicks who swung into action then, the chair in reverse mode she manoeuvred her charge away from the bed, steering him swiftly toward the narrow doorway.

Outside in the corridor they waited, dumbstruck as Nurse Carter settled the ranting patient before joining them.

"Take no heed of him, Sir," she addressed Mr. M directly. "It's the trauma, hallucination. And it's worse on the night round, the screaming and sobbing- they're all battling with their demons Mr....."

As she came to an abrupt halt Edward who had been hiding behind Anna's skirts strode forward. "Mr Mystery," he said. "Mr A Mystery."

The awkward silence of a moment ago was lightened as everyone laughed out loud and Nurse Carter made a polite curtsey before the nameless stranger, whose name at this present moment in time seemed irrelevant. Then the pretty young nurse stepped aside and spoke in a whisper to the doctor.

"Don't worry Lawrence, if he were aboard the Rohilla on that fateful night, someone with some degree of sanity, will certainly remember."

Whatever her faults, Hicks was at least thorough. Kate disliked her intensely but her attention to detail, according to her father was unique. This morning for instance their subject was Geography. One hundred and one facts about the African subcontinent, the climate, the people, resources all lodged in their notebooks and duly learned by rote. Meticulously planned and completed not a minute short of the stroke of noon. However, although Maria Hicks had been at number thirty two for all of two years neither Kate, nor her sister Florence had developed one grain of respect for the perfect governess.

And so despite the chill weather and promise of rain it was with some relief they could now escape the torment of the schoolroom.

The square was unusually lively even for a Saturday afternoon. It was late October and the day had been fine so far but now an inky blue sky threatened yet another storm. Kate peered into the windows as they passed, eager to look at the new fashions and stare at the elegant ladies while Edward struggled with the wicker shopping basket Mrs Dawson had entrusted him with. Inside the basket, Kate knew full well there was a written note and a set of instructions. He was to visit Mrs. Munton of the fisher community on his way home to purchase a bunch of Valerian root.

This small task was eagerly undertaken by Edward. His main aim in life since his arrival was to be of some use in the household, prove his worth and make a name for himself.

Mrs Andrews had provided a suitable diet for Mr M in accordance with Dr Hinton's instruction and although this had no doubt improved his physical health, it had done little to ease the ongoing nightmares. The Pickering's housekeeper had been a customer of Ma Munton' for years and spoke highly of her magical 'Valerian Tea.'

Anna was there to meet them by the White Horse and Griffin, eager to show them her new studio in the bustling square. It was a momentous day, something she had been looking forward to since her arrival in Whitby, the one glimmer of hope to lift her from her recent bereavement. She was lively of step and there was a rosy blush to her cheek that Kate hadn't seen before.

"It's not a large premises, but it's quite central. Plenty of room for storage and the views from the bay are spectacular, great for the water colours," she was saying as they walked.

Most of her conversation was directed at Mr. M who eagerly asked questions; when the studio would be opened and what hours she intended to trade. Kate had never seen him so animated, as they moved swiftly through the little streets and onto the square.

Kate's perceptions were keen this morning as she fixed her gaze on Hicks. She couldn't help noticing the emerald gleam in Hick's eye as it lingered on the pair in deep conversation. There had been the sly glances before, the disapproving way she raised her eyebrows, clicked her tongue.

The frivolity of the occasion was further fuelled by Mr M's bright mood as he commented on his diary, where he noted the small steps to regaining his memory. His anxieties, each minor recollection and marvelling at the joy of the past few weeks in the company of the Pickering family and their ongoing hospitality. Kate witnessed the change in Hick's mood as Anna opened the door of the little studio and ushered her guests inside.

"I start tomorrow, early morning sketching then opening hours, ten till five. It's what I've always dreamed of, what David and I saved for all those years," she told them.

“And the customers will come, there’s no doubt about it, in there hundred’s…thousands even,” enthused Mr M. Kate was sure that at any moment he could just rise from his chair and walk, dance maybe so great was his enthusiasm. But there was a stony silence from Hicks who swung the wheelchair round on the spot and clicked on the brake.

For a moment they paused, surveying the little shop, starkly bare, with only a handful of Anna’s painting propped up in one corner and a dilapidated table serving as a counter. It was cluttered with all manner of brushes, paint pots and tubes of water colours. Several large packing cases stood by the back door unopened. Anna passed round tall glasses filling them with water from a huge glass jug and stood back with relief, her opening speech delivered.

Mr M gazed at Anna admiringly, the weary look that had haunted him that evening on the Nab was all but gone replaced by a relaxed and natural smile. Kate was pleased for him, happy that at last he was beginning to respond, unperturbed by the horror of his ordeal, the outspoken patient who’d dammed him at the hospital or the slow and taxing search for his missing memory. Kate recognised in him a great warmth, and a determination to overcome all the obstacles, the very qualities that she herself possessed.

“Thank you all for coming, for being my first customers…I don’t have any champagne or tea or anything but I am very grateful for your opinions and support.”

Mr M turned full circle, the rubber tyres screeching to a halt on the slatted floor. He examined the contents, sniffing the bouquet, admiring the colour then savouring the palette.

“It doesn’t look much just now…but in time, given your unique talent and a bit of hard work, I know the business will blossom,” he raised his glass.

Kate and Edward raised their glasses in agreement and everyone cheered including the reluctant Hick’s as Anna thanked them again. As they left, their host turned to address them again. She told them not to be strangers; to call in whenever they were passing and to spread the word to potential customers.

“And you John,” she said looking straight at Mr. M with a mischievous grin, emphasis on the newly claimed Christian name. “I think a portrait is in order, when can you come for a sitting?”

Kate wasn’t fooled by the smile on Hick’s face just as she didn’t fail to notice the way she pretended not to hear the last remark.

Mr. M was silent a moment taking in the meaning of Anna's words. Kate could see the workings of his mind, his innermost thoughts as he struggled to find an answer.

"But I though you… worked on landscape. Isn't it kind of difficult to paint a vacant face…. a man without a past, a name, a true identity? "

Anna closed the shop door behind her, replacing the bunch of keys in her pocket and began to walk. As she took one more look at her dream, the dream that she and David had saved for together it was almost as if she were walking away from the past and moving on to the future.

"No John, I don't usually do portraits but there is change in the air and who knows it may be a new start."

Edward was distracted. He'd also been asked by Mrs Dawson to call in at the smokehouse for fresh kippers and some fresh eggs from the grocer but as he started down Henrietta Street his attention had been drawn over the red slated roof tops to the bay.

Kate watched as he dawdled by the sea wall watching the little gathering of fisher folk. It had been a constant fascination for him, since he'd arrived in Whitby and whenever he got the chance he would sneak down to the shore to watch the children mending the nets. Kate always knew where to find him.

"Edward," she said "Haven't you been for the fish yet, you know how mother loves them."

Her cousin didn't answer. He turned on his heel, kicking a loose stone from the path and made for the curing shop. A strong woody scent greeted them. It hung in their nostrils, permeated their clothing and it made their mouths water.

After purchasing four pungent portions of herring Edward made for the foot of the church steps, leaping and whistling a tune gripping the aromatic parcel as he crossed the crowded street. Darting down the narrow alleyway to the sea he disappeared from view. Kate shouted, her voice was carried by the wind but it was lost in the dissonant cry of the seabirds. She followed speedily, desperate not to lose sight of her young cousin. He showed no fear, always trusting but he was an innocent and furthermore he couldn't swim.

Kate peered round the corner of the building, the stone walls were cold beneath her fingertips and she felt the crunch of sand beneath her boots. Edward was scrutinising the few pennies he had left in his hand, creeping closer to the corals, where the nets lay idle and the sand was coarse and firm. Several fishermen were hauling boats up from the water's edge, their woollen ganseys flecked with spray, their brows creased from the strain and a few fresh face women sat mending the nets.

Edward examined the loose change then replaced it in his pocket. His eyes were now firmly fixed on a young girl not much older than himself, wiry and lean in a woollen skirt and tartan shawl. Bent over the fine meshwork she sang, the nimble fingers sorting squirming bait into a copper pail. She didn't look up as he approached but continued her song in the clear northern twang, a haunting melody, a sea shanty.

Kate knew the girl was aware of his presence, he had after all been there before, silent and curious as only a young city child could be. In light of earlier experiences, she also knew the girl could not be trusted.

After a few minutes the work was complete and she stopped singing and got to her feet.

"What have you there, boy?" she asked, a wild look in the slate grey eye.

"Just kippers for my aunt's tea," he told her.

"Kippers for tea eh?" she mused, looking him straight in the eye.

"They cost so much...... an' now I haven't any money left for eggs and Mrs Dawson wishes to bake a cake, tomorrow," Edward informed her.

Kate remained where she was, hidden from view but ready to intervene if the need arose. She had never trusted the fisher children with their dextrous fingers and beady eyes, touting for pennies and scrounging in refuse bins.

"No matter, boy. Here's a nest for kippers," she said, forming a seaweed basket on the wet sand. "Lay two o' your bonny fish in there and tomorrow you will have some kipper eggs for your trouble."

A buxom woman sitting close by shifted her heavy skirts, raised her eyes to heaven and shook her head.

"Come on boy...you still have two more fish, don't you?" the girl coaxed.

The paper parcel in Edwards hand was still warm, and he gripped it tighter as he considered the girl's advice.

Kate watched him, straining her ears in an attempt to catch the conversation, but again the voices were lost.

The little band of workers began gathering their lines, retrieving the well-stocked buckets in readiness to leave. But the girl was undeterred, embroiled in the mischief of the moment she nudged Edward's shoulder her broken drawl prompting action. The buxom woman raised her voice again and this time Kate could clearly sense her angst.

"There's nay much he does' ne see," she called to the girl.

In seconds the decision was made and Edward ran forward, opened his packet and placed two of the kippers in the makeshift nest the girl indicated. He tucked them in neatly, licked his oily fingers and re-wrapped the remaining pair. Retrieving his shoes he inserted the paper package beneath his arm and then was gone like the wind, over the sand and onto the side street. Kate feared Edwards errand was less than accomplished; only two fishes remaining, no eggs and his promise of Valerian tea for the gentleman completely forgotten.

"And so young Edward, what is the matter with you today?" asked Mr M.

The recovering patient had been wheeled to the very edge of the beach as near as the Kate had managed to get the wheelchair. She felt his every irritation these days, not just the physical pain but his innermost feelings - the growing desire to be stronger, more independent, manage his own thoughts. Here he could watch the waves hitting the shore, catch the scent of the ocean and feel the salt spray on his face.

In his eyes was a light Kate hadn't seen before. As though a tiny spark had ignited deep in his brain, kindling a specific event, a snippet of memory a brief moment in time to give him hope.

Edward shrugged, running bare feet through the fine sand and trying hard not to cry.

"Nothing, Sir."

"Your tears tell me different, young Edward," he persisted.

In the past few weeks they'd shared stories, walked together, talked together and although Mr M was battling with his own anxieties he was quick to notice the emotional changes in others. Edward too had been suffering, his mother ill and his father called away to war. Kate recognised the fellowship between them, the man and the boy, sharing their sorrows.

Edward sighed, looking up at the affable features, now mirroring his pain and wiped away a stray tear.

"T-was' the kippers, Mr M. They didn't lay the eggs," he said.

Mr M threw his head back and roared with laughter, the juddering wheelchair giving rise to some concern. Hicks came running from the sea wall to check the brake, and Kate replaced the fallen blanket as Edward leapt onto the top step afire with indignation.

"Why it's not funny, Mr M....Mrs Dawson, she was waiting for them eggs so she could bake a cake....and I hadn't enough money left to buy them."

The laughter subsiding Mr M leaned over, taking the small boy's hand in his and straightening the crumpled collar of his sailor suit.

"I'm sorry Edward, you're such a tonic."

As they headed back toward the West Cliff they made a detour to the grocers to buy the fresh eggs. It was an easy way to remedy the situation. It didn't however ease Edward's embarrassment at his own gullibility.

He was silent now, and Kate imagined he'd be thinking about the timely trickery, how the scheming minx of a girl had hoodwinked him into providing the family's supper.

But it seemed his mind was on other things as they crossed the bridge.

"Aunt Anna says you can't remember anything about before...before we found you," he said. "Where do you think your memory has got to?"

Mr M did not answer for a while and Kate feared that Edward had touched a raw nerve, prodded the deepest most painful wound of all. Hicks hesitated on the bridge, the green tinge evident in her eye at the mention of a certain name. A hooter sounded in the bay and they all looked out to sea.

"I think, young Edward that my memory is out there, somewhere," he said. "Out there in the vast ocean. But every day the seagulls spread their wings, they visit distant shores, the farthest horizons, the deepest lagoons, searching far and wide....and one day Edward I know for sure they will return it to me."

Kate hovered between stairs. She often sat here in the late afternoon listening to the banter of the young housemaids and feeling the warmth of Mrs Dawson's kitchen. If she swivelled her head she could glimpse the narrow passage that led to the back door, where local tradesmen called with their deliveries, then directly below her the kitchen and staff dining room. Then with a little manoeuvring she could peer through the left hand bannister and see the laundry room, tucked neatly between the larder and boiler room, where Kate could catch the heavenly scent of clean linen.

She gleaned so much more than she ever could upstairs, snippets of gossip, first hand, not adapted for juvenile ears. All the excitement of the supper table, news from the front not to mention the talk of secret liaisons.

"Oh, my Mr.Grigg," Mrs Dawson was saying. "Dr Hinton has requested we serve a wider variety of fruit, wholegrain cereals and a daily dose of Valerian Tea for the gentleman. Young Edward must have forgotten to enquire about it, and now I'll have to contact Mrs Munton myself," she drew breath and began again.

"If it isn't hard enough getting the basics at the moment. I've nothing against the mystery gentleman and I do hope he makes a swift recovery but I just don't know where it's all goanna' to end."

"Makes my life much harder I can tell you," came a more familiar voice. "In the schoolroom all morning, with no time to plan lessons and out all manner of places come afternoon."

Kate could imagine the stark features, the cold, calculating eye and the resolute chin. She shifted uneasily on the stairs, the hairs rising on the back of her neck as she strained to hear the ongoing conversation.

"He's a dark one alright, can't trust him an inch.....a criminal no wonder, a thief, a conscientious objector, who knows. Or even a deserter. "

CHAPTER 5. Lou's story – 2014

Lou was running, faster than he'd ever run in his life before. His heart was pounding in his chest, his lips were parched and his mind was taking a guilt trip. If only he'd been there for his sister, hadn't left her, seeking his own selfish pleasures, shirking his responsibilities this would never have happened.

He took short cuts through yards, jarring his shoulders in narrow passageway and tripping over loose paving stones, without stopping for breath. A concerned Nette followed behind struggling to keep up and calling for him to slow down. He was oblivious, demented, waiting for his whole world to come crashing down at any moment. It had all got out of hand and now he was about to pay the price.

As he turned the corner into Church Street Lou was aware of the flashing police car situated at the far end. He stopped, panting, a cold sweat gathering on his brow. Two police officers got out and began making their way up the cobbled street. Lou watched as they marched by the busy shops and minute cottages. Goths posing for photographs, children clutching bags of sweets. Everyday people, doing everyday things, none of them remotely aware of the advancing officers or the nature of their business

"Lou" Nette said, stopping abruptly.

"Slow down….I'm sure you've got this all wrong."

Moving forward a few steps he stopped again, fumbling for the key in his jeans pocket. With any luck someone would be in at the B and B if they hadn't all gone out searching. His mind was in a turmoil as he grasped the fob firmly in his hand, like a good luck charm, a talisman.

Lou had slowed to a steady walking pace now, eyes firmly fixed on the uniformed pair, his breath coming in short bursts like a bicycle tire with a slow puncture, the familiar street sounds drowned by the tread of regulation issue on the irregular patch. The officers were on a mission, not making house to house, interviewing locals, they had a fixed destination and Lou knew exactly where that was.

He quickened his step again, driving his way through the crowd, with Nette in pursuit arriving at the B and B as the officers were rapping at the ramshackle door. They paused a moment by the perilous porch, peering through the grimy windows and wrinkling their noses as they exchanged glances.

Lou came to an abrupt halt. He struggled to say something but the words just wouldn't come.

Aware of someone behind them, the officers turned about.

"You staying here, Sir?" the younger of the two enquired.

Lou looked over their heads his immediate concern beyond the threshold.

"Lou Bannister" Nette volunteered, impulsively "He's here for the Goth fest, with some others."

The officer nodded, moving aside aware of the urgency in Lou's eyes and his eagerness to get inside.

"I believe you are from the Pudsey area…?"

But Lou was already turning the key in the lock, entering the precarious porch desperate to avoid the revelation that he knew was to follow.

"I believe so…." said Nette, trying to fill the gap.

At last Lou was in, straining his vocal cords in an effort to arouse the occupants.

"Anyone here? Ellie….Ellie!"

In an instant she was there, slightly flushed, a little breathless but amazingly alive and well.

"Where the bloody hell have you been?" he blared.

"Well, I could ask you the same thing, Lou," she said, hastily fastening the top button of the low cut T shirt in honour of the official looking guests.

They stopped abruptly, oblivious to the unconventional array of tenants gathered on the stairwell. Even the unwelcoming smell of mothballs and the bizarre ticking that accompanied Dag failed to draw attention.

"Can I make tea for anyone?" said Perdy, peeping round the kitchen door.

It seemed there was a teenager missing, a Simon Granger from Pudsey. The police officers passed round a school photograph, a little worn at the edges and taken at the beginning of the autumn term. Lou stared hard at the print, the uniform was distinctly Crawshaw High stock but the face was unfamiliar.

No one at the B and B recognised the boy and although Lou could easily relate to what his parents must be going through he couldn't help feeling a huge sense of relief. Thank God Ellie was safe!

"We'd like you to keep your eyes and ears open if you would," the younger officer was saying. "Any clue at all would be helpful at this stage…..just give us call."

"You sure you're Ok Lou? Nette was saying as she picked up her guitar and the tattered newspaper she'd managed to salvage.

"Yes, yes.....I'll be fine," Lou assured her, his mind still elsewhere.

He leaned absentmindedly on the precarious porch as he spoke, eyes still hollow and bloodshot from last night's liquor.

"Well, if you're sure...maybe see you around then," she said.

Slinging the guitar strap around her neck she left without a backward glance.

The headache was lifting, the double vision returned to normal and a couple of hours kip meant Lou was feeling better. If only he was here without Ellie. He was young and single after all, he could do what he wanted, see who he liked and no one could stop him. He'd told his dad he was looking for a job.....why not. The accommodation was cheap enough, the nightlife was great and well, Ellie wouldn't be starting college till next Easter.

And then there was Nette - Yeah, they'd only just met but there had been some connection and each time he thought about her he had that strange melting feeling deep inside. She was easy to talk to, a good listener and she'd been there for him when things were at their worst.

Then he realised that in the heat of the moment, when he thought his world was going to crash around him, when he was at his lowest ebb, he'd forgotten to check out her mobile number.

"Lou!"

He heard the voice but it didn't register.

"Lou." It came again accompanied by a tapping.

Ellie entered edging her way onto the rickety bed beside him, her simpering voice a harsh wake up call.

"Retch can't make it, he's gone down to see his brother in Derby," she sighed.

"I need to Skype him at seven but can't seem to get a signal. Can you fix it Lou?"

It wasn't a great deal to ask Lou supposed and it may help to ease that lingering guilt complex.

"Ok Sis, leave the tablet here. Soon as I've had a shower I'll have a shot at it."

It was cold as usual in the sparse little room and Lou shivered as he thought about occupying the draughty bathroom, with the dodgy shower head and blind-less windows.

Only three thirty and the light was fading. He'd pinned back the cobweb curtains to make use of the remaining daylight outside but it only served to emphasise the bleakness of the place. That all engulfing mothball odour still lingered and although the tap tapping had stopped Lou had been unable to discover its source.

Whatever the B and B lacked in comfort it certainly made up for in terms of Wi-Fi, the signal had been amazingly strong since their arrival so Lou was at a loss to understand what had caused the problem. There certainly hadn't been a power cut and unless Ellie had dropped the tablet it should still be functioning.

He pressed the iPad button and waited to see if the screen lit up. It took a few seconds but eventually it burst into life. At that moment Dag appeared at the door, the tall gaunt figure looking uncomfortable in the stark surroundings and to Lou's dismay the screen blanked out. With his roommate's arrival came the tapping sound, that hollow rhythmic beat that he'd found so aggravating on their first meeting.

"Hey man, kinder dark in here," he said, flicking the nineteen thirties light switch and flooding the room with an intense light.

Lou flinched, shielding the screen from the intrusive glare. He clicked on the Skype icon and waited, in anticipation. It was taking an age and the sound of Dag rummaging in the little drawer by his bed was decidedly annoying.

"What's that tapping? It's driving me mad," snapped Lou.

"Just the timepiece, man, it's what makes me tick,"

A lack of amusement showing on Lou's face he returned to the tablet, clicked the contacts icon and then onto "Retch". He clicked and waited again. If the device wouldn't work this time maybe he'd just go look for the router and plug in there.

"It has to be here somewhere….." Dag continued, digging deeper into the little drawer.

Lou was beginning to feel tetchy now, it didn't take much granted but Dag hadn't exactly made a good impression since his arrival. He was noisy, irritating and his obsessive sense of orderliness was becoming intolerable.

"Can't it wait…..I'm trying to get a signal here," Lou snapped.

Search suspended for a moment Dag retrieved the offending article from the hallway, placing it on the end of his bed he smothered it with the pillow.

"Sorry, Man, usually stow the old ticker away but can't find the lock for the cabinet."

Lou looked round frustrated now but a little curious as Dag uncovered the timepiece again.

"Oh, right…it's a clock then?" Lou said. It was a question that Lou wished he had never asked and one that was to shape the events that followed, and indeed, his very future.

Instantly Dag was the showman, exhibiting his intricate showpiece, demonstrating its vital parts. It was certainly a curious instrument, the likes of which Lou had never seen before, a set of bones, a metal skeleton, a mechanical torso, without a face.

"It's our life Man, ticking away the minutes, the hours, the weeks, the years. Marking our time."

He talked quickly, describing each individual part, the gleaming brass cogs, the balance wheel regulating the movement, the delicate hairspring every component with a vital function in order to create a precise and perfect movement.

The sound of Dag's voice and the metallic beat had a strange hypnotic effect on Lou but the Karma was short lived as Dag returned the timepiece to the top of the chest of drawers and resumed his search. The background noise was becoming intolerable, maybe the hangover still lingering. Bloody thing thought Lou, enough to drive you ape, can't he just sort it.

"For God's sake Dag!"

His roommate immediately silenced, Lou returned to his task. Within seconds it seemed his roommate was reunited with the missing lock and he retrieved the gadget from the chest and struggled to imprison it.

But now the tablet was coming to life again, the Skype screen alight, bursting into action once more. Lou clicked on 'Contacts' again, then 'Retch' and immediately the link was active.

He moved closer to the screen, listening for a voice, trying to establish contact. He had a picture at last though slightly hazy and if he pressed on the microphone icon he was sure he could make a connection.

Peering at the screen he focussed on Retch's dingy flat, the tatty furniture and worn carpet. Last time Lou had been there he'd tripped over a dozen empty beer cans and the sink had been filled to the brim with dirty pots, but today it appeared a little tidier. He could just see the steps descending, as he remembered, to the hallway below. But the picture was frozen and no sign of Retch.

"Hello…"

Lou frustration mounted as he fiddled frantically with the volume panel.

There were shadows at the edge of the screen and a bright ray of light reflected in the mirror, but the room was totally empty.

"Damn it" he yelled.

The door was flung open and Ellie stood there waving her mobile in the air.

"It's Ok Lou. I got through to him…can't make it tonight but he'll be here for the party next weekend."

Lou shook his head in exasperation, typical of Retch, let her down again, what a surprise.

It wasn't purely by chance that Lou stopped by the beach the next day. Now the sun had come out and although there was a slight breeze it was pleasant enough for a walk. It wasn't just coincidence he thought, that the solitary siren had ventured that way too. Lou had recognised the faded sandals by the steps, the lingering perfume and her haunting melody.

Nette wore a scarlet fleece today, her softly flowing locks framing the radiant face her eyes lighting up as she watched him approach. He ploughed on over the beach, ignoring the sand that trickled over the top of his loose trainers and joined her on the rocks.

"Hi Lou," she said slowly, as if savouring his name. "How's Ellie?"

Lou shifted closer, loosening the zip on his jacket in response to the midday sun. He blinked, nodding a response, as he remembered their first meeting here just hours ago and the way she'd made him feel.

"She's good. Just missing her boyfriend."

Nette had that air about her, he thought, a certain confidence, that 'everything will be alright' look that seemed to wipe away any trace of worry. He liked that about her and the way she made him melt inside.

They walked along the beach, through the square and up the steps all one hundred and ninety nine of them. Then they strolled round the churchyard, onto the abbey and took the little hawthorn lane back to town.

Lou told Nette about his parents, their demanding occupations, the trials of chaperoning his sister and keeping an eye on her social circle. His sense of isolation, being trapped, unable to lead his own life.

It felt good to talk, to know someone was really listening, someone who could turn a negative into a positive, a frown into a smile, with just one look.

"You worry too much, Lou…..don't take life so seriously." She reached out touching the flushed cheek gently, generating the growing inclination he had to, sweep her up in his arms, to hold her. Then she grabbed at his collar with both hands, pulling him gently toward her teasingly, before releasing him.

"Ease off, Lou, take a break, Ellie's a big girl now," she said.

He forced a smile, maybe she was right….hadn't Kalen said more or less the same thing?

Wasn't it time he stopped grousing and started taking control of his life?

"I'm down at the pub tonight if you're free, we've a special show, bands from all over Yorkshire," she was saying.

Lou stepped out of his trance, straightened the screwed up collar and watched her walk away. For once he was speechless. Even though they'd only met the day before he felt the wrench, a parting pang and he knew now that she felt the same.

The fire was burning brightly in the shabby living room, lifting the mood of the chilly October day. Despite the early despondency at the less than adequate accommodation the atmosphere at the B and B was lifting. Everyone had gathered to celebrate Merle's birthday. As a true Scorpio she was often detached and isolated from the group but with her man by her side she revealed her true self, the passionate, plucky peacemaker.

Even Ellie had made an appearance, Lou noted as he levered the ring pull on his Stella. She too looked chilled, stretched out on the chaise longue with Midnight draped purring over her stretch denim legs, her hair gleaming, finely manicured fingernails stroking the soft fur. She and Perdy had been good friends from the start, even in the early days, swapping make up hints and scanning the girly magazines, their schoolgirl giggling keeping Lou constantly informed of his sister's whereabouts. All keyed up for a night at the Spa, they checked the tickets and discussed their favourite acts.

Hathus was in full swing, witty and dynamic as ever reeling them in with his wise cracks and smooth talk; the girls entranced, the guys amused but unconvinced. His eyes alight with the telling, his expressive hands in motion, presenting, spinning the yarn.

Lou basked in the warmth of his huge personality, the velvety voice, memories of punchlines past as he hovered near the bookcase scanning the titles absentmindedly. He was beginning to relax now, beer in hand, Ellie safe, and his love life looking up.

There was an impressive finale, followed by an explosion of laughter as Hathus wound up the tale, flexing his tattooed arms and raising his glass to his appreciative audience.

Amid the uproar the door flew open and a slightly flushed Perdy entered, her hair concealed under a makeshift turban, her modesty covered only by the skimpiest of towels. She shivered in the doorway, smelling of freshly shaken talc, a mixture of wild flowers and lavender.

"Somebody in….in there!" she announced.

Stopping abruptly she surveyed the company, acutely aware of her blunder as she grappled with the inadequate drape.

The moments that followed was punctured with the vocal concerns from her housemates as they tried to calm her.

"In the bathroom," she said breathlessly. "Some thing or somebody – in there."

It was sometime before they managed to calm Perdy, carry out a thorough search of the bathroom and convince her that she'd imagined it all. Lou of course had had his share of unease here, the strange odour of mothballs, that cold clammy feeling in the cellar but he kept his thoughts to himself. The last thing he wanted now was to spook Ellie.

The weather had been unseasonably mild for the time of year, the sea smooth like a millpond and though Lou had ceremoniously donned his jacket before setting out he was finding the warmth of the open fire somewhat overwhelming in the small taproom. Loosening his collar he made for the bar.

He ordered a beer and moved into the jostling crowd that filled the seafront tavern. It was brightly lit, bursting with character and served an array of local beers. Lou had looked in on Ellie before making his move. She and Perdy were heading for the Spa and were heavily embroiled in their usual beauty routine, He'd left them haggling over pots of glossy varnish and face creams with strains of Coldplay in the background. It was easy to slip away, Quilon out at the Seafarers again, Kalen making plans for Saturday's party and the rest of the bunch getting ready for a night on the town. He was feeling remarkably calm, liberated from his usual duties, free to do whatever he desired.

Glad of the lively venue yet delighted to be solo for a change, he was looking forward to the entertainment. He could hear the scrape of strings from the adjoining room, the tap of a finger on a microphone and the rasping voice of the compere as he welcomed everyone.

From where he was standing he could see straight through to the next room where the punters were packed tightly waiting for the Band to strike up.

It looked like a special occasion, the walls trimmed with bunting, people waving Union Jacks and Lou could see a huge poster on the wall, with a sepia print of a ship in distress on the rocks. It drew Lou's attention as did the enchanting melody that filtered through the throng. The voice was unmistakably familiar, haunting and sincere, the song of a sea siren.

'A stormy night in Whitby bay

A biting north east wind and swirling rain….'

Lou's jaw dropped. With the local brew as yet untouched in the glass, he suddenly felt light headed, strangely inebriated, euphoric even. He moved forward depositing it on the nearest table, negotiating the narrow doorway he slipped through into the crowd.

'And his blood runs cold, a ship has run aground.'

Nette glanced up as she sang, holding his gaze just briefly before joining in with the chorus. The poignant lyrics held him, filtering through his being, filling him with a strange apprehension, as his heart beat a little faster. It was like that sense of wonder you feel at the top of a mountain; the awesome view, the shock of the altitude and the acute realisation that one slip could send you over the edge. Yet, somehow you know there is no going back.

The East bay took on a different appeal this evening, a warm breeze fanning them and the soothing sound of the tide turning, effervescent lines of white foam lapping lazily on the shore and stars that mesmerised them.

They left solid ground discarding their shoes, swapping the firmness of the quayside for the velvety coolness of the sand. They paused, scanning the shoreline, watching the tiny waves rippling the water's surface, causing the cobbles to rise and fall, stirring their creaking timbers into a gentle rhythm.

Lou held Nette's hand tightly as they raced along the beach, each alive with the moment; charged by the generous glasses of the local ale they'd consumed. Reaching the rocks, smooth and comforting, breath coming in small spurts they sank down, thankful for the familiar sanctuary.

Lou watched Nette as she stared out into the night, her face illuminated by the moon's silvery glow. It wasn't just the drink that had affected him, or even the way she looked at him with those wide expressive eyes but somehow at that moment he knew life would never be the same again.

"It must have been so terrifying out there for them…… so many hours, with the wind and rain lashing …not a welcoming light or any hope of rescue," she reflected.

Lou was deep in thought, he heard Nette speak but the words washed over him. He knew he should get back to the B and B and check that Ellie was tucked up in bed, lock and bolt the doors, sleep off the hangover. And yet he couldn't take his eyes off her. He homed in then, drawn back to the sadness in her voice, the significance of her story, the look on her face.

"It was out there, the Rohilla….floundering on the rocks, so many drowned, so many brave, innocent people."

Nette recounted the night of the disaster with a strange clarity, the storm that lashed the decks, the helpless victims who met an untimely death and the struggles of the local people as they rallied to save them.

"My Great, Great Grandfather was on board, "she suddenly said. "He was one of the lucky ones."

Lou was touched by her emotion, her concern for those affected by the tragedy so long ago and he reached out and took her hand. A cool rush of air caused him to move closer, cradling her in the crook of his arm, her perfume filling his senses like the incoming tide. He looked deep into her eyes, noting the tear that coursed the brow of her cheek and the smile that played the corner of her lip. There was that melting feeling again, stirring deep inside him.

He wiped away an escaping tear and slipped his fingers through the honey gold hair to the smooth of her neck beneath, gently drawing her toward him. There was an urgency now, an all- consuming need to possess her, to lay her down in the soft, seductive sand and strip the mermaid of her scales. He felt the arousal, heard the murmur of her consent and the pressure of her body against him. She was beautiful, intelligent, sensitive and most amazing of all, she was focussed on him.

But this wasn't the spirited Suzie, the lascivious Jessabelle….this was Nette.

Instantly he drew away, fearing he'd read her wrongly. He didn't ever want this moment to end and yet one false move and all would be lost, the spell broken and Nette would slip back into that deep ocean never to be seen again.

And then instantly, she was gripping his collar, reeling him in again, teasingly, tantalising. She ran her fingernails down his back, tracing the curve of his spine, rounding his hips before kissing him with a passion. Lou responded, feeling the urgency, and watching as her fingers wrestled with his shirt buttons. He felt the warm breath on his face, drank in her perfume and they fell silent, slipping onto the awaiting sand.

CHAPTER 6. Lou's story – 2014

It was getting dark. There was a certain hustle and bustle in the house, sounds of an IPod blaring from one of the bedrooms, a chink of crockery skimming the sink and someone snoring below. Lou walked briskly through the hallway past Ellie's room, the female frivolity from within giving the reassurance he needed. It seemed his sister had finally settled in. Having enjoyed last night's line up at the Spa and slept late she appeared relaxed in Perdy's company and miraculously for the moment all thoughts of her missing mate had evaporated.

Lou was beginning to chill too. The scruffy Tee shirt he'd taken from his holdall, un-ironed on his back told the tale. The prickly stubble, razor shy on his chin went unchallenged and he'd left his bed unmade. He smiled to himself as he reached the back door, events of the previous night still crystal clear in his memory.

Opening the door he emerged into the sun dappled yard, where the last of the daylight was fading. It was his intention to seek out his old mate, Quilon though he doubted he'd be around. Summoned to duty, likely returning only at dawn to sleep it off. It was a busy time of year at the hostel, preparing beds, serving soup and offering emotional support to those less fortunate. Seemed a poor way to spend his vacation and though Lou wasn't unfeeling or callous in any way he wasn't going to play second fiddle forever. After all they'd a lot of catching up to do.

"God, you startled me…"

Lou looked round, momentarily stunned, letting the door slam shut behind him. His old school chum was almost a mirror image of himself, unshaved and un-pressed. The crumpled jeans and tatty oversized vest clinging pathetically to his portly form revealed the too tanned torso beneath. He couldn't help grinning at the notion.

"Hi….thought you'd be long gone. Bit of a loner these days aren't you?" Lou said.

Quilon shared their odd likeness with a knowing wink, checking the time on his mobile and briskly heading for the gate.

It had been two days since their arrival and apart from the barbeque on the first night had been noticeably pre occupied. He raised a hand in greeting, screwing up his eyes at the last of the sunlight and flicked a strayed strand of hair from his forehead. His face was decidedly pasty, Lou thought, eyes bloodshot and heavy lidded.

"Where you kipping then, mate?" Lou fished, peering round him and into the cellar below. He was sure all the rooms within the house had been taken, apart from the attic which was out of bounds.

“Below stairs, Mate…..didn’t want to disturb no one.”

Lou noted the inappropriate luggage he was dragging behind him, a Nike gym bag bulging at the seams and a Khaki overcoat. He slung it over his arm, hoisting the bag onto his shoulder.

“Seems you had a great time at the Bar B Que, Mate,” he paused, grinning.

Lou wondered what Gaz knew about the missing hours, the scathing comments which were surely shared afterwards and felt his face flush.

“She’s a cool one that Jessabelle. Just one of Kalen’s little inducements...eh?”

Lou changed the subject hastily. “It’s a grand job you’re doing Mate, everyone says so. Catch you for a beer later then.”

Quilon paused shifting the heavy load and turned about.

“Hey, Lou, how about coming down with me, see how they work down there, lend a hand….we can grab a beer later at the Griffin.”

Lou looked shocked, he hadn’t expected that. His mind wandered briefly, contemplating an arranged date that very evening with Nette. The beautiful, intelligent and utterly amazing Nette. The softness of her skin, the honey gold hair, the way she made him ‘melt’ inside. Still he could call her, ask her to make it tomorrow.

“Err, sure.” he said, though he wasn’t sure at all. “I’ll grab a jacket.” The big arched doorway opened before them, casting a lamplight’s beam from the street into the gloomy interior as yet another ghostly figure entered. Keeping bills down was the first priority of the volunteers as they set to work in semi darkness in order to save on electricity.

A second priority was warmth and so as soon as the door had been opened, it was instantly shut again. A white collared gentleman patrolled the entrance ushering individuals inside, one at a time, offering heartening words and pointing vaguely in the direction of the kitchen.

Lou stood behind the trellis table, ladling thin soup into metal bowls and handing out a single slice of bread to the incomers. The faces he looked into were vacant, unmoved by the action, the mouths mostly silent as they devoured the bread almost before it left Lou’s hand. The line was moving rapidly now, young and old, fit or infirm they elbowed their way in, desperate for the meagre sustenance.

On receipt of their supper they moved rapidly to the far end each grabbing a slip of paper with a printed number on it. Without exception they bundled it hastily in a pocket or down a trouser top as though it were a fifty pound note. A whiff of unwashed flesh mingled with stale tobacco caused Lou to recoil momentarily.

In a corner of the lacklustre room were a number of trestle tables, quickly filling up now, metal clattering on metal, an odd lack of conversation; the diners' only intent on filling their bellies.

Lou had never seen anything like it before. There'd never been a day in his life when he'd felt that sort of hunger or ever a time when he hadn't had a roof over his head. He shuddered watching the shuffling band of drifters emerging through the church doors, one after the other, snaking across the dusty floor in search of possibly the only meal they would consume that day. He felt ashamed, his hand shaking as he estimated fair portions, whilst longing to serve more.

"Grand job you're doing there, Lou," said a voice from behind. Quilon was heading for the dormitory with a mountain of fresh sleeping bags in his arms.

"Yeah, mate no worries."

Lou found himself looking into the eyes of a young boy, maybe six or seven, his blonde hair tousled and his features masked by a layer of grime. He was sure he'd already filled his bowl moments earlier and yet how could he possibly ignore the desperate plea. This wasn't some sequence from a Dickens' novel, this was here and now the twenty first century.

Lou's hand trembled, the bowl refilled and before he could regain control of the ladle the urchin had vanished.

It was gone ten when the kitchen finally cleared, not a single morsel remaining and a sink full of dishes. Quilon talked, animated, while stacking them on the drainer, his voice echoing round the stone interior.

"It's not the lap of luxury, Lou but at least it'll tide them over. Social worker will be here tomorrow and hopefully some of them will get something more permanent."

Lou scanned the room. Six tables set for breakfast and chairs neatly tucked under. Everything done to military precision and not a crumb in sight on the flagged floor.

"So...what happens if they don't get here for seven thirty when the doors shut?" Lou asked.

"Locked out I'm afraid, there's nowhere else within miles…."he said "There's a place down by the quay, they gather down there, light a fire, swap some backie. If they're lucky, it won't rain."

Lou thought about the wild North Sea, the storms that racked the coastline and the bitter winter temperatures. He couldn't imagine how anyone would survive the night out there in the elements at this time of year.

"And the children?" Lou continued.

"They're subject to the curfew just like everyone else....if they don't make it they sleep rough and go hungry for another day, they've no choice."

After they had packed away the remaining dishes Lou helped Quilon tackle the trellises, folding them neatly against the wall ready for the morning.

There was a click of a latch from the rear of the building as they crossed the floor to leave.

"Thanks for that lads, it makes such a difference...all tucked up now and not a peep till the morning."

Reaching the arched doorway they looked round. It was the white collared gentleman, his face drawn and sketched with wrinkles, testimony to his taxing day.

"See you tomorrow then, George and take it easy. They'll be fine, winds' dropped and pavements are dry as a bone," Quilon assured the vicar with a broad smile.

"Your right of course they're all in God's hands. Thanks again, lads." And he raised his eyes to the ceiling with reverence and smiled wearily, yawning as he shut the door firmly behind them.

The beer was cool and so welcoming, slipping down easily, soothing away the remains of the last particles of dust from the church's dry interior. Lou was pleased to sit down and although the public bar was crowded they relaxed into a reminiscent mode. Reliving those sacred schooldays, wild summer vacations, the parties and the girls.

"Well, how you doing at the B and B Lou? There a mixed bunch aren't they."

"Yeah," Lou agreed. "No change there - completely crazy but wouldn't change them."

Lou took another gulp of the local beer and frowned.

"B and B's OK, nothing special, barely standing actually but that's not a problem least we have a roof over our heads. Just that weirdo I'm sharing with...you know him at all?" he added.

Quilon's eyes glazed over, Lou tried to read him but his face was a blank. Fleetingly he looked away distracted maybe by the leggy blonde collecting glasses. His attention resumed, his response was swift.

"Dag, you mean.....all and out Steampunk, got it bad man and stinks into the bargain. Glad I'm not bunking in with him."

Lou shifted in his seat, the noise levels in the popular bar increasing as he strained to catch the conversation. Quilon raised his voice, knowingly and continued.

"He's a dark one, up to something ...wouldn't trust him that's for sure. Just watch out. Got an eye for your sister if you ask me."

Lou's thoughts raced. Ellie, he'd forgotten about his sister......at the B and B at that very moment, almost midnight and that freak wandering about. Bugger this babysitting lark, he fumbled in his jeans pocket for his mobile knocking the beer sideways, froth spilling over onto the polished table top.

"Hey mate.....steady on!!" Quilon shouted.

There was a message flashing on the screen but Lou ignored it....tapping the contacts.

He touched on Ellie's number and let it ring, oblivious to the stir he'd created in the crowded bar. Quilon steadied the glass and pulled out a paper hanky, dutifully mopping up the spilled beer acutely aware of the negative attention they were drumming up.

By now Lou was frantic, no response and only an answer phone message available. He got to his feet, scraping the table across the beer splashed floor and headed for the exit.

"What about your pint, man," Quilon called after him, apologising forcefully to adjacent customers, who'd caught the shower.

Lou was already out the door and striding purposefully down the narrow street, clutching the mobile to his ear and mumbling instructions into the phone.

"Stay where you are, Ellie," he was saying. "Don't go anywhere...I'm on my way."

It was with some relief that Lou fitted the key into the lock at the Band B as female voices drifted from the bedroom above.

Christ, thought Lou did they ever stop? What did they find to talk about into the early hours?

At least Ellie was safe and sound, even if she hadn't bothered to answer her mobile. Still he wasn't about to tackle her on that score tonight, the local brew was definitely stronger than the piss they served in Pudsey and besides he was knackered.

The feeble light that emanated from the cracked lantern above his head, barely supporting the task as he groped for the handle. He entered the precarious porch sighing with relief as he ploughed on into the hallway. It was bitterly cold, even inside, the last remnants of the fire still smouldering in the living room grate as he passed by. No late night revels tonight it seemed, lights extinguished and only a few scattered cans lying dead on the coffee table.

Lou crept toward the stairs, guided by the single shaft from the landing window. He heard the grandfather clock sound in the back parlour, a pathetic chime, the creak of its workings heralding its age. As he mounted the stairs, a final toll of the clock accentuating the silence. He paused, acutely aware of another sound. The bedroom door was slightly ajar, swinging on the creaking hinges and from the interior a distinct scuffling noise.

The voice that followed was familiar but distinctly distraught.

"Arrrgh!"

Lou pushed open the door to reveal Dag's, slight form, a dancing silhouette, shouting obscenities, visible only in the mottled light seeping through the cobweb curtains. The hum of moth balls hit his nostrils like an incoming tide.

"You evil critter, you devil. Wait till I get hold of you!" yelled Dag, stumbling forward feeling his way in the darkness.

Suddenly the blanket on the nearest bedstead fluttered and a black, shadow emerged, eyes like amber spotlights piercing the gloom.

"Midnight?" Lou stepped aside to let the frenzied feline pass.

Squawking and hissing it dived through the open door, fur flying, ears erect, seeking escape.

"Hey! Hey!" Lou tried to calm the situation, grabbing Dag by the arm as he skidded across the polished floor in pursuit of the terrified cat.

"It's only Midnight."

He peered out into the hallway checking the cat had made its getaway, pushing the door to before turning to confront his roommate.

"For God's sake, Dag what the hell's going on?"

He located the light switch, the single bulb revealing the dingy digs and the skinny steampunk struggling to release himself from Lou's grip.

"Bloody mangy cat…..I'll skin it alive if I catch it in here again!"

Lou scanned the small room still missing the point, trying to grasp the situation. He stood between Dag and the door, the all and out Steampunk pacing the floor, his face crimson with rage and his fists clenched.

"Don't know what your problem is mate……only a darned cat, wouldn't hurt a flea, scared of its own shadow," Lou spoke slowly, breathing deeply, slinging his coat haphazardly on the bed.

He watched as Dag made for the set of oak drawers, wedged in the narrow alcove his fingers working furiously with the brass handles. He pulled the top drawer open forcefully, slipped his hand inside and drew out a small transparent box. Lou moved closer, his interest aroused. He'd avoided the drawers, dreading the green mould that spotted the top and had left his clothes in his travel bag.

He gasped. Inside the small casket, maybe five inches square and in desperate need of a duster, Lou could just make out the body of a black arachnid easily the size of a matchbox and covered in a thick jet black, fur. For a moment Lou simply stared, not that it was anything unusual to keep a spider as a pet, but the discovery of this third occupant in the room made him just a little bit apprehensive. Instantly the hairs on his neck prickled and his hand went automatically to the offending spot.

"Now my little darling, you're safe this time," Dag glared into the glass house and lifted the lid, poking a limp finger into the cube to check for signs of life.

Lou flinched, Boa's, Rattlers, venomous Vipers no problem but spiders gave him the creeps, not to mention their owners.

"Tell your sister to keep that cat under control," Dag nodded in the direction of the landing. "I'll have it next time…….me and Simba, we won't tolerate it."

Lou had toyed with the idea of bunking in with Quilon, in the cellar, cold as it was down there at least he wouldn't be troubled by peculiar pet owners and he'd have the place to himself most evenings. But he resigned himself to spending as little time as possible with his crazy roommate, zipping his sleeping bag up to the very tip of his head to avoid any nasty night encounters.

He phoned Aunt May, just to check on Butch and asked her to report that there was nothing as yet on the work front and they'd be staying on a little longer.

In his preoccupation with the new delights of the B and B he had completely forgotten to contact Nette. Monday morning, as he crept from the bowels of his sleeping bag, he noticed the stray text on his mobile from the previous evening, timed at 7.30 pm.

How had he managed to miss it?

Wasn't it impossible to erase the evening they'd spent together? The softness of her skin, the honey gold hair, the way she made him 'melt' inside.

His first reaction was to respond, apologise profusely and promise to make amends, but he knew that wouldn't wash with Nette. She deserved better.

No, the only way was to go right down there and confront her. Tell her how he felt, set her aside from the Susie's and the Jessabelle's of this world and sweep her off her feet, before someone else did.

Lou took a shower, put on his best Tee shirt, the one with the lizard motive, the stonewashed jeans and jacket. He glanced in the mirror checking the razor's efficiency and dabbed on the aftershave. He called at the florist on the way and cradling a bunch of red roses he took the small alleyway that lead directly onto the sea front, as the gulls screeched overhead, wheeling toward the bay where the tide was high.

Lou suddenly stopped, doubting that Nette would even be there at this time of day. He sighed, exhausted a feeling of defeat creeping steadily over him.

The far rocks were indeed empty, the narrow stretch of beach deserted and dark clouds gathered overhead.

He'd go to the house, bang on the door until she came, shout up at the windows, call through the letterbox………………And then he realised, he had simply no idea where she lived.

CHAPTER 7. Lou's story – 2014

Walking back through the narrow walkway, he sneered at the redundant roses passing them over his shoulder like a deflated Dick Whittington. He tried desperately to recall their conversations, their talk of family, friends, the local area.

Did she live somewhere on the West Cliff?

Or here in one of the little terrace cottages lining the harbour?

Why didn't he call last night, tell her he couldn't make it and arrange to meet her another time?

What made it worse, he'd inadvertently wiped her contact details from his mobile.

How could he have been so stupid?

Emerging into the square, he looked around indecisively. The shops were closing now for lunch now, stallholders on the market tucking into sandwiches and steaming coffee and shoppers making their way home. A few children lingered by the sweet shop, dipping into their bags of spice and calling names. Lou swerved to avoid them and continued up toward the main street. An ageing accordion player continued his rendering of Danny Boy as several stray dogs howled in appreciation. He glanced over at the Goth market and set off across the square, his breath laboured, his pace quickening,

Then he began to run, despite his fear that she could be lost to him forever, a fleeting affair, a holiday romance, doomed from the start.

Then he heard a voice. It seemed to be coming from the tiny shop on the far side of the marketplace. Lou turned abruptly, straining to hear above the rumpus in the street.

"Lou! Lou!"

He approached the brightly lit studio. The pretty exterior was awash with colour, terracotta flower pots and huge swags of bunting stretched across the windows. A wrought iron table and chairs to the forecourt completed the chocolate box image. The shop door was slightly ajar as he approached and still unsure if his ears were playing tricks, he stopped to listen again.

"Lou, just hang on a second….I'm on the phone," came the familiar voice.

He obeyed, ducking through the miniature doorway, narrowly missing the "at lunch" sign that hung there and winding his way through an array of huge boxes that lay opened on the shop floor.

Inside, the whitewashed walls were completely ensconced with vibrant prints, sunny seascapes, views of the abbey and a number of charming portraits that drew Lou's immediate attention. He skirted the room, transfixed by the startling display of characters, local bigwigs, elegant ladies, innocent eyed children and, by the door, a set of Gothic ghouls, the Steam variety, Victorian Gothic and Cyberpunks.

He moved mechanically along the display, inching his way toward the counter.

"Yes, I'm on with it now, dusted down some of last year's stock and I'm just going to price it," the phone call continued. "But there's someone in the shop…..I'll have to go."

Lou heard the ping of the mobile as the dialogue ceased and a door opened behind the counter. At once Lou's attention was diverted, his brain working overtime in an effort to form his excuses.

"Oh, I thought she'd never stop. You'd think we were expecting royalty the way she goes on," Nette was muttering as she appeared in the doorway.

She stopped, smiling - an audible sigh leaving her lips at the sight of the flowers.

"Hi Lou. I'm so sorry, I just couldn't make it last night. I've been up to my eyes in it here," she was saying, dragging him back to reality.

His response wasn't immediate, caught up in her apologetic announcement and the spectacle of her appearance. The beauty that stood before him now, could outshine any of the females displayed here in the gallery, even with their individual charm and grand clothes. The high cheek bones, radiant complexion and glowing eyes momentarily dazzled him, putting the fateful moment off when he would lie to her again.

"Thanks, they're beautiful."

She took the roses from him and went out back to put them in water.

Careful now, he told himself…don't cock it up. Maybe, just maybe he was getting a second chance.

"Well I can see, you've got your work cut out," he called after her, playing for time as he glanced around at the overflowing packing cases.

Nette lifted the hinged section on the counter and came toward him, smoothing down her crumpled dress and taming the golden locks that had strayed.

"Yes, I've another three out back to sort. Now the Goth's have up and gone we need to appeal to the typical tourist."

She stood less than a stride away from him now, surveying the ominous assignment in front of her. Lou wanted to reach out and touch her, ease the pressure posted on her face, offer some words of support but the moment was gone. Nette was already tackling the boxes, easing out the topmost frames and dusting them down with an expert hand.

"I tried to text you but my credit was low…."she continued without looking up.

Get too it Lou, he prompted himself, don't be a complete idiot.

He abandoned the denim jacket, revealing the lizard motive and releasing an over exuberant application of aftershave. If he moved quickly, maybe he could just salvage the situation, make the right moves, say the appropriate things, and create an impression. It wasn't too late, surely.

Eventually, all the empty packing cases lay neatly folded by the back door and the substitute stock in pride of place. Nette had returned a number of vibrant watercolours to the window and replaced the Goth memorabilia on the forecourt with a collection of the typical seaside post cards.

"Thanks for that, Lou," she said, touching his shoulder in a way that sent shivers down his back and caused that familiar melting again inside him. "I'd never have done it in time without you."

He watched as noting the time on her mobile she flicked the "closed for lunch" sign to "open" before returning her gaze to Lou.

"No problem, really," he answered, dusting down the lizard motif as he joined her at the door.

"I came to ask you to the party Saturday night…..just our little gathering, you can meet Ellie properly then."

There was a long pause before Nette replied and Lou struggled to read her response, behind the fixed smile the clear but cautious eyes.

"Oh, I don't know Lou, it's not as though I know them. I'm not sure if it's my scene."

She glanced through the window at the little crowd of customers gathering by the post card stand and she opened the door. Lou wondered now if all his hard work had been in vain.

Was she going to dump him there and then?

Had he actually read the whole situation wrongly?

After all she wasn't a Suzie or a Jessabelle. Surely, this couldn't be just a one night stand.

"I'm sorry, Lou I'll have to go," she said, slipping through the minute doorway to welcome her customers.

A backward glance as he reluctantly left, seemed to confirm his fears as she didn't look up but carried on with her shop keeping role. He blamed himself of course. How could he forget their arranged date, not a phone call not even a text to let her know, he'd blown it and he had no one else to blame.

As soon as Lou grabbed the door handle he could feel the vibration as the whole house seemed to shake, like the aftershock of an earthquake. His hand trembled as he turned the key and entered the hallway. The noise was deafening and he clamped his hands to his ears in a vain attempt to block it out. An angry Hathus was poised at the foot of the stairs, roaring like a lion and banging his fists on the bannister.

"Give us a break, Dag for God's sake!"

The deep baritone voice although powerful was no match for the agonising din that was coming from the floor above. Lou recognised the pulsing discord of Siouxsie and the Banshees, infiltrating the very rafters of the B and B and causing the remaining residents to assemble behind the gentle giant in his impossible mission to silence the monster.

With some frustration Lou retrieved his key and placing a hand on the big guy's shoulder he mounted the stairs.

"I'll deal with it." he shouted above the din.

An orange glow oozed from the partially open door way at the head of the stairs. Hands still firmly pressed against his ears Lou moved tentatively forward, silent but seething at his insensitivity, his lack of thought for the other guests not to mention his roommate.

At last he was peering around the door, trying to focus on the scene within. He shifted his position to bring the occupant into line with his restricted view and moved closer.

Dag sat cross legged on the bed like a petulant pixie, head bowed, that distinctive scent of mothballs still heavy in the air. He seemed to have no awareness of the sheer volume of music coming from the two amplifiers laying on the opposite bed. The metal stud jacket and jet black jeans gave the impression of a giant beetle, feelers poised and working quickly, undoing a small brown parcel.

Unaware of the observer he lay the crisp paper out on the bedspread, smoothing the sides out to reveal a small plastic bag. Lou's eyes widened, he tensed, the innermost part of his stomach contracting like a spring. The startling white substance was unmissable in the overhead light, dazzling in fact, its purpose unmistakable. Dag leaned closer eyes glued to the contents, a haze suddenly drifted over his eyes as if its magic was already working.

"A fucking smack head," Lou said, words lost in the growing frenzy of the CD.

Lou couldn't believe it. Sharing his room with a junkie and with Ellie just down the corridor. At that moment Dag turned his head, as though he had become aware of a presence, covering the conspicuous white substance with the manila packing he scooped it up, depositing it in the top drawer of the chest. He looked round nervously before scrunching it up and sliding it inside next to the little beastie.

Lou made himself scarce. He didn't want to challenge Dag there and then, he'd bide his time, keep vigilant and in the morning get the hell out of here. Seems Quilon had been right all along and the sooner they were on the road home, back to sanity the better. Despite the lateness of the hour when Lou finally got his head down on the moth eaten chaise longue Lou slept like a baby. His sleep was broken only by the chiming of the grandfather clock in the hallway and it was only as it chimed ten that he opened his eyes to see a scantily dressed female figure loading two cups onto a tray in the recess that was the kitchen. She deposited two heaped spoons of sugar into each before replacing the milk carton in the fridge.

"Oh.", she said in surprise as she caught Lou's eye. "Bugs in the bed?"

It was a second before the Heineken head cleared and he could determine the familiar curves of the gregarious redhead as she floated, goddess like toward him. Lou had to admit she was a stunner, the striking features, a figure that would grace any model walkway and a sparkling personality to boot. But though she had many admirers and no shortage of bed partners, it was clear she only had eyes for Kalen.

Lou forced his eyelids open, attempting a smile.

"Perdy…thought you were a burglar," he said, grabbing at the escaping blanket that threatened to reveal his naked state.

"Tea in the pot if you want one…or maybe it's the black coffee for you this morning," she jested, grabbing his big toe and giving it a teasing twist.

Lou groaned, tucking the abused toe back safely under the cover. He reflected on the early morning conversation he'd had with Hathus before he'd finally drained his glass, the over large frame jammed up against him as he tried to keep his eyes open.

"What you really doing down here?" she persisted, "it's not the most comfortable of settees."

She was right of course, much worse even than the old bedstead upstairs, but Lou seemed to be a master of deceit lately and he answered spontaneously.

"Can't cope with the snoring."

"Right….." she raised her eyebrows giving him a sympathetic pat on the head as she turned to leave.

"Oh, by the way Lou, Ellie and I are going into town this morning, we're looking at something romantic in the Victorian line for the party on Saturday."

Suddenly Lou's head was clear, working overtime on their getaway plan, their break for sanity. After all there was no point in staying now, he'd blown it with Nette and Quilon, was out of it…doing his bit for society, God Bless him. There was just no reason to remain in Whitby now the festival was over.

He sat bolt upright, like an indignant meerkat.

"Well, not sure if we'll be staying Perdy….you know, Ellie needs to get back she's promised to do some stand in work for Dad before she starts college and……."

"Oh, she didn't say Lou. I thought at least we were all going to be here till Sunday."

Lou stuttered as the excuses came out together with an acute twinge of guilt as he anticipated Ellie's reaction to the news. After all hadn't he been the one who'd persuaded her to come, almost dragged her along and now when she'd settled, developed friendships, got into the spirit of things, now he wanted to go.

"Our lord and master won't be pleased you know," she said the cups teetering on the rim of the tray as she stopped to register her disapproval.

“He’s down at Tesco as we speak, ordering the grub, raiding the liquor section….wouldn’t be in your shoes, Lou when he hears the news.”

Typical of Kalen, Lou thought, liked everything in order, everyone at his bidding. But he caught the mischievous streak that flashed across her face before she turned full circle, steadied the tray and slipped through the door.

The bedroom door was slightly ajar as he entered the corridor, the heady aroma of Chanel filtering from within as he stopped to listen. There was no sound, only the sharp blast of breeze assaulting his ankles as he drew closer. Someone had obviously left the window open, in their haste to leave. He nudged the door open and looked in.

The room was empty, with that ‘just vacated’ feel as though at any moment there would be a tap on your shoulder or a voice in your ear. Lou could only presume the two of them had gone in search of costumes regardless of the conversation earlier and possibly with Ellie still unaware of his plans to leave.

He leaned over the dressing table. Reaching up he grasped the upper latch firmly, easing it down the splintered paint flakes spattering the windowsill below. Hovering by the window, he could just see Perdy and Ellie tripping down the pebbled driveway, lost in their girlie gossip and oblivious to the resounding thud of the window above. They turned the corner in a fit of giggles and disappeared from view.

Lou sighed. He’d have some task persuading her to leave now, he knew that, not to mention Kalen’s reaction to his decision.

He turned, abruptly deflated, his breathing suddenly laboured and his chest tight. It was reminiscent of the adolescent asthma, long dormant yet not forgotten. His throat tensed, eyes pricking he stopped in his tracks.

The classic print of the floating lady above the bed held his attention again before his eyes came to rest on Ellie’s little bedside table. There in a crystal vase, startling in their very simplicity and presented with perfection were a mass of scarlet poppies. Lou’s eyes filled up, his nose itched and he knew he should remove himself from the obvious cause of his symptoms. But curiosity got the better of him. This was no idle passion of Ellie’s, a fleeting fondness for the local flora, a desire to be closer to nature. It just wasn’t her style.

Beneath the crystal vase, on the highly polished veneer was a ripped corner of a grimy cigarette packet its surface covered in some indecipherable scrawl. Lou moved in, ignoring the mounting irritations as the only legible word flashing warningly in front of his eyes. DAG xx

"Shit," Lou muttered out loud, circling the bed as a shower of scarlet petals slipped silently to the surface below.

Was this just a one off gesture? A meaningless offering? Or a cheap chat up tactic? And if that was the case, was the attraction one sided or was the feeling mutual?

This was the worst scenario imaginable, Lou thought. Why did Ellie have to fall for one loser after another?

Lou felt breathless as he reached the hallway, his throat contracted his eyelids tight and uncomfortable. Somehow the corridor seemed so much longer than normal - his steps insignificant, breath shallow and rasping. Little droplets of cold sweat emerged from his brow, his fists clammy and clenched involuntarily.

"You OK, Lou?"

Lou stopped in his tracks, brain jabbed by the familiar voice but unsure of its owner. He turned to see Merle, still encased in her dressing gown and clutching a wicker wash basket, containing a collection of smalls that hardly promised respectable coverage.

Before he could answer he was wracked with a fit of coughing, gasping for breath he leaned against the bannister.

Merle paused, concerned. She dropped the basket and moved closer.

"No, I mean you look terrible," she said abandoning the washing and guiding Lou toward the living room she hastily deposited him on the chaise longue.

"My God, what's happened?" she continued, loosening the buttons on his cotton crew neck. "Breathe steady Lou, real slow now."

She ran toward the kitchen area the sound of cupboard doors hammering and shifting of crockery adding to the chaos. In seconds she'd returned with a paper bag which she held out to him, shades of the school playground on PE day and as far as Lou was concerned, not a moment too soon.

"Breath into that!" she yelled, the timid, unassuming Merle suddenly finding a voice.

It was some minutes before Lou felt his heart steadying and the colour returning to his cheeks.

"You gave me a real turn then Lou, are you feeling better now."

She fluttered around the room, opening windows and providing cushions before sitting next to him on the threadbare chaise longue.

"Yeah,Yeah," Lou nodded vigorously, embarrassment setting in. "It's nothing really."

Merle fluttered her all too obvious eyelashes, nervously shaking her head.

"Didn't look like nothing to me?" she argued.

Lou had never really taken an interest in Merle before, for one thing she wasn't someone that grabbed his attention.

She was of small build, slight with deep brown eyes and a short crop of raven hair. He noted the sharp rasping voice rising now as she registered her concern. The timid sensitive Blackbird, steadfast, loyal and wholly devoted to her long term hero, Hathus.

"It was the flowers set it off, the ones in Ellie's room."

Merle sat upright beside him, a puzzled look contorting the birdlike features.

"Poppies, they don't usually bother me but maybe the pollen counts' high just now." he explained.

Lou started to get up. He was feeling a little self - conscious and not wanting to encourage further sympathies from any of the other residents he planned on a swift exit.

"Oh, Poppies…..they're not a good omen."

"Not a good omen?" he repeated. "How do you mean?"

Looking as if she could have bitten her tongue Merle stopped fussing with the cushions and went to close the window.

"Not a good omen for me obviously…."Lou barked.

Merle stood perfectly still now and Lou wondered if he'd upset her but she continued filling him in on the gloomy detail.

"Hathus calls it the flower of death, red petals symbolising the blood," she informed him soberly.

Crazy these Goths….thought Lou, always looking on the grim side, courting doom and disaster. They seemed to thrive on it.

"Ah…blood," came the baritone voice from the doorway.

Lou realised that his hasty exit was likely to be thwarted as they turned to see the long term hero, glistening and golden following his workout at the gym.

Merle tried to play it down and Lou could see she didn't want to make a big issue of his childhood allergy so he played along.

"Just a minor cut nothing to worry about," he said grasping his thumb tightly and making for the door.

"Hey, mate. Perdy tells me you're taking to the road; it won't be the same. Sure you can't stay till Sunday?"

Before Lou could respond the gentle giant turned, distracted by the mounting commotion from the hallway.

He slipped to one side as it opened once again, to reveal the almost anticipated trio, still bubbling with enthusiasm from the recent spot of retail therapy....Perdy, Dag and Ellie.

Lou's jaw dropped. It seemed his chance of getting away was swiftly fading, like the threadbare chaise longue, the bedraggled B and B and the prospect of a long term lover.

His amazement was not all to do with the dynamics of the trio but the sheer magnetism of the visual spectacle before him.

Perdy came as no surprize. Her scarlet she devil costume, exaggerating the hourglass figure, with a resplendent Dag in the guise of Edward Scissorhands but in the centre of the trio and drawing the most attention was Ellie.

Lou had never seen Ellie like this before. She was his kid sister for goodness sake, impressionable, naïve and vulnerable. Yet somehow in the past few days she had turned into a young woman. The exquisite ebony costume she wore fitted like glove, a crisp crinoline that could have been individually tailored to complement the perfect figure and sun starved porcelain features.

"Ellie..." Lou couldn't find the words.

She stood motionless, a satisfactory smile lingering on the pretty face as every eye in the room was drawn toward her.

There was a kind of expectant silence, watching, waiting willing him to speak.

"It's no big deal brother.....me and Perdy have just signed up to do the Christmas rush at Boyes. We get payed weekly and there's a bonus when we're done at New Year."

Before Lou could totally take in Ellie's last remark the door opened again, this time to reveal an informed Kalen. The word on Lou's departure had obviously got out. He felt the critical eye, the laser look, focussed not on the celebrity trio but directly at him.

In the excitement of the evening and with a million chores Kalen had saddled him with, Lou had little interest in sorting out a costume. Fancy dress wasn't his thing anyway, dressing down was more his style jeans, tee shirt and last year's trainers. In the end he set himself up as a fairly mediocre monk. It was a compromise, just like the agreement he'd made with Kalen. He might as well resign himself to the fact that there was no way now that they would be leaving before New Year.

He'd play it cool as usual, resume the chaperone role, drink a few beers and maybe, just maybe he could find some seasonal work till after Christmas. Obviously he'd blown any chance of any lasting relationship with Nette so come the New Year he'd simply cut his losses and they'd head home. His only concern at this moment in time was the little "crush" Ellie had recently developed for the dopey Dag, and it worried him. They were sat on the chaise lounge together now, Ellie sporting a coy smile and Dag tapping his scissor tips on the wooden armrests as he ogled the conspicuous cleavage.

Lou bristled, he had thought things couldn't get any worse than the witless Retch. But, Ellie seemed to have resigned herself to the fact that he would probably never turn up.

He just hoped that his sister's new liaison didn't develop overnight, so to speak and resolved to look forward to a time when then they would be gone, back to the sanctity of predictable Pudsey.

With the music loud, the alcohol flowing and the party in full swing Lou shifted uneasily in his seat. He needed some air. Most of the revellers were crammed into the narrow hallway, in small clusters. A few local punk followers hanging onto the remnants of the bi annual festival joined them, their ticket a random bottle with dubious content. Several scantily dressed Cyberpunks clung to the lower bannister, as Lou brushed past toward the front door. Strains of heavy metal vibrated in his ears as the DJ slapped on another Bauhaus disc.

Lou noted Quilon's presence. He'd obviously forgone his volunteering duties tonight in honour of the occasion and was making the rounds in his very authentic vampire suit.

Through the stained glass Lou could clearly see a silhouette. Another gate crasher no doubt, brandishing yet another suspicious liquid and already well oiled. The place was heaving; the flashing strobe sending out a welcome to every passing piss head; the suspiciously, heady mixture of tobacco smoke endorsing the invite. He was concerned that the rising decibels would antagonise the neighbours, who in turn would summon the police. Dag was making his way to the nearest loo, the sound of the steel fingers rattling across the banisters, set his teeth on edge. He stepped into the porch, leaving the inner door open whilst debating whether to let yet another lunatic into the fray.

He reached the door and opened it abruptly, ready to deter any further undesirables.

In the aperture stood an angel, a sight to behold, silent and radiant, the mere hint of mischief reflected in her eyes. The company was hushed in an instant, music killed, the strobe stilled. No one moved. It was the expectancy of an eclipse, the calm before dawn, the aftermath of a storm.

"Nette…"said Lou.

Dag stepped forward, his jaw dropping involuntarily, the hairy tarantula slipping from his parted lips. It dangled there dramatically without an eyebrow raised.

Nette remained hesitant, framed in the doorway, a perfect picture. As she did so a strange phenomenon took place, a remarkable illusion. It was something Lou would never forget. A shimmering light gathered momentarily, sparkling, dazzling above her head, forming a veritable halo. Quilon roared at the sight, shielding his eyes from the glare, the canine molars revealed.

The illusion fading, Lou's eyes descended to the threshold, taking in the bareness of her sandaled toes, the pure white of the translucent dress and above to the gossamer tresses that enveloped her chaste form. He was about to say more when Dag, quickly concealing the strayed arachnid pushed him to one side.

"Oh, we have an innocent in our midst," he gloated, eyes like saucers scouring the bare legs and heaving breasts.

"Who's your mother then...the Virgin Mary?"

Intrigue of the moment spent, the spectators speedily removed themselves and Lou, eager to resolve the situation, made a dash for the door. But Nette was gone, spirited away - the evening chill the only remaining entity to remind him of her visit.

CHAPTER 8. Kate's story – 1914

From where she was sitting - her forehead wedged against the bannister - Kate could just see the unlikely pair. Hicks tall and steeple like, shoulders set; her form forbidding even from the rear - her curly headed cousin, like a trapped animal, wedged against the back door. The note that passed swiftly between them and the tuning fork finger vibrating deliriously before Edward's troubled face stirred a deep unease within her.

Aware of the little errands Edward had undertaken lately, trips to the grocers, simple kitchen chores from Mrs Dawson; Kate sensed his need for a purpose in life. His eagerness to please was endearing, but this new phase, as Hick's hired hand, hinted of deceit and that truly troubled her. She flinched, watching his escape, the scrap of paper stuffed carelessly into his side pocket. Brushing past the starched apron and dodging the huge hands he made an abrupt bid for freedom.

It was chilly in the stairwell and Kate shuddered as she dislodged herself from the oak framework, taking a step backward into the shadows so as not to be seen she hid until the coast was clear.

It had been several weeks before 'John' felt able to make the appointment at the studio and today was the day. Several parcels of clothing had arrived, suitable for a gentleman of some standing, which Hicks was asked to deliver to the guest room. Kate followed her along the corridor as she stopped for bath towels and clean linen for the patient's bed. The laundry always smelled of fresh lavender, soft and smooth to the touch reminding her of the times she and Florence would assist Mrs Dawson with the hanging out. Her reverie was short lived though as they turned the corner and entered the empty bedroom.

Kate had pondered by the guest room door watching as Hicks removed a pinstriped suit from the package to lay on the counterpane. It was of smart cut, slim fit with buttoned cuffs and the trousers were neatly pressed. The white fitted shirt and patterned cravat were complimentary to the outfit and the previous owner, whoever he was, obviously paid good attention to his wardrobe.

Kate could see the hostility in Hick's face whenever she reflected on their visitor, the glint in her quick eyes, the puckered brow, the taut lips and that deeply disapproving look. Their own relationship with the formidable teacher offered little better - an education by rote with a highly inflexible syllabus. She and Edward hardly dared utter a word in the schoolroom except in response to a question and woe betide either of them if their notebooks were incomplete or their handwriting untidy.

Mr M had been well enough to sit downstairs for some days now. Fresh faced, smoothly shaved, reading the local news and jotting down his returning thoughts from time to time. Then settling down to enjoy their youthful company before the afternoon saunter along the seafront.

It was Anna who escorted them today and Kate was longing to visit the studio. She loved the brightly coloured canvasses adorning the white washed walls, the local scenes of sea and shore. Places she knew and had grown up with, skilfully drawn and preserved for all to see and admire. How talented her Aunt was she thought, so skilful in her craft and her paintings showed so much attention to detail.

As they turned the corner into the square, a chill wind hit Kate's cheek, reminding her that winter was closing in and, pulling her wool collar closer, she fished in her pocket for mittens.

Of late, Edward had taken to walking some paces behind and today was no exception. Glancing over her shoulder she caught sight of the straggler, red cheeked and nonchalant, jumping the cobbles as he strived to keep pace with the others. Ever more curious about the note concealed in his pocket, Kate resolved to keep a look out for her cousin who seemed recently to be dicing with danger.

Grey and bleak as the little market place was on that winter afternoon, with a blustery wind and the crashing breakers on the nearby shore it still held a distinct appeal for Kate. She ploughed on pausing briefly at each storefront to gaze at their wares - her attention divided between the glitzy window dressings and her wayward cousin.

Anna was in command today, cheerful and charming and somehow more radiant than Kate had seen her since her arrival in Whitby. It had been eight months since her bereavement and even Papa had commented on the lifted mood. Grief had of course touched them all, leaving a void within the family and a feeling that nothing would ever be quite the same again.

Kate had also noted the unusual lightness of her Aunt's voice as she stepped out, the way the sun enriched the gold in her hair and coloured her previously pale complexion. And how she now wore the customary black band on her right arm, in place of the former mourning dress.

The little studio was soon ablaze with light as Anna wrestled with her easel, in order to achieve maximum light from the low windows and be within reach of the counter storing the brushes and pencils. There were a couple of sturdy packing cases which served an audience quite admirably and Kate was quick to occupy one. The reluctant Edward hovered in the doorway as Mr M wheeled himself as instructed to centre stage. Occupied then with her artist tools, Anna turned her back, her mind visibly racing with artistic notions, advising the sitter in terms of his comfort and posture.

“The light isn’t too good but I’m only working an outline to start with, head upright, eyes forward. You’re absolutely fine where you are….”

As she turned full circle, Anna gasped, her pencil falling with a clatter to the floor below. The dropped implement drew both Kate and Edward’s attention and they all looked on in amazement.

A broad smile transformed Kate’s face as she beheld the patient, free standing beside the invalid chair his legs strong and stable, shoulders back, chest out. He remained there a moment as though awaiting applause then slid onto the wicker chair by the window with an air of relief. His triumph was acknowledged by a loud cheer as Anna smiled. Shaking her head in disbelief she bent to retrieve the pencil.

Neatly groomed, smartly dressed with a clean complexion, the distinctive mole a surprisingly appealing feature, Mr M had a certain unique and spellbinding charisma. It was truly an amazing transformation.

Kate’s memory of that night following the storm, the first encounter with the wild man, clinging to life, his fate at the mercy of the raging sea. At that moment it seemed like she had dreamed the whole episode, awoken from a nightmare for she could find no trace of that bygone being in the man that stood before them now.

Instantly the spell was broken as Edward, exuberance restored, ran to his side reaching up to fling his arms around the mended man.

“Mr M…” he cried burying his curly head in the broad shoulders.

There was a wave of excitement as Kate joined them and Anna business like as ever brushed a stray speck of dust from the pinstripe lapel and re-positioned the proud chin.

In Kate’s eyes the mystery man was now the epitome of the perfect gentleman, a pillar of the community, respectable in every sense of the word…she believed in him, admired him and most of all she recognised in him certain characteristics that she herself possessed.

There was a brief silence as the children returned to perch on the packing cases with renewed interest and Anna relocated the easel. She moved forward with purpose, running her hand over the smooth canvas the pencil poised for action.

It was then that the subject spoke.

“It beats me why you would want to paint a…. nobody, a man with no name just a vacant face and fancy clothes.”

For a second Anna didn't answer, so deep in thought maybe with her eyes firmly fixed on her tools of trade and not on the sitter. Then she blinked, the winter sunshine stalling her for a moment, bringing her sharply back to the realms of reality. A strange look passed between them and Kate became anxious, concerned that the sitting would be abandoned. She held her breath, biting her lip as she awaited her Aunt's response.

Anna moved quickly now, arranging herself directly in front of the sitter, hands on her hips and her feet in stubborn mode. She replaced a loose lock escaping the jet black comb that flattered her face and she spoke with a passion.

"John Mystery....you are the perfect subject, you have style and charm, a wonderful sense of humour and most of all you are real."

Kate admired her aunt's forthright manner and her determination. It was true that since the loss of Uncle David, Anna had lost that sparkle, appearing despondent with a certain melancholy in her eyes, but now the mourning veil was lifted.

"I can wear all the finery, play the jester, captivate a queen but that's just a front, a false facade, an acting role," he continued, voice raised and the pain of imperfection displayed on his brow.

Anna moved forward leaning over the reluctant model's chair, the caring hands gripping the smoothness of the arm rests as she looked intrusively at the troubled face. She lifted his chin again as if addressing a small child and Kate a saw a deep compassion rising from within her.

"John, we all have an external mask that we show to the world, it's who we'd like to be, desire to be and we never stop trying to reach that goal. There's no sin in striving," she informed him.

"And, besides which, John Mystery, I have a certain intuition as an artist....I know for certain you have a true heart and when I look deep into your eyes I can see your very soul."

If Kate had mastered the unique skills of her aunt, she would certainly have captured the scene framed there in the shop window. The mellow sunlight, the rapt figures, the transient emotions, would have created a most moving masterpiece.

Yet the moment had passed, with a remarkable healing process taking place, which Kate felt sure was of a mutual benefit.

They left the studio at four thirty and strolled down the little jetty on to Tate Hill Sands. It was peaceful there, the wind having dropped to a whisper in the distant hilltops, the sea calm and serene in the setting sun. There was no one in sight along the stretch of sand only a gathering of seagulls at the far end of the pier. Kate had collected a few loose stones from the fringes of the rock pools to attract Edward's attention but the ploy hadn't worked and the light was quickly fading.

Anna summoned them as she steered the wheelchair round a stray dog that came from nowhere onto the beach, streaking down the pier in pursuit of the gathered gulls. It barked frantically, startling the little flock and coming to an abrupt stop at the end of the promontory. Disillusioned it turned, flopping to the ground in defeat, an industrious paw scratching at the tousled fur.

"Come on now, time to go," came the call from Anna again, strikingly clear in the evening hush.

Kate was reluctant to leave, instantly drawn to the stray dog, having finished its ablutions now staring reflectively at the farthest point of the pier. The liver and white body shook vibrantly scattering the loose hair from the scratching.

"Yes, Miss Kate. It must be time for tea..." said Mr M in that strange but unrecognisable drawl that had recently become so familiar.

Kate and Edward watched, fascinated from the sand's edge, as the mangy mongrel remained fixed to the spot, unmoved, his eager eyes scouring the beach. He pricked an ear, senses alert, his body in readiness. He was keenly focussed on something in his line of vision as a pathetic whining emerging from the drooping jowls.

Then without warning, in one mad dash, ears flying behind him and with a profound sense of purpose he raced down the pier like a bat out of hell, a bullet from a gun, a fox with a pack of hounds on his trail. It was difficult to see the distraction; a mischievous moggy maybe or an anxious owner demanding his attention.

Within an instant it seemed, the determined mutt was beside them slinking round the wheelchair and rubbing against the checked blanket, jumping up, his paws plying for attention from the surprised occupant. The pitiful whining continuing as Anna tried to calm the situation, shooing the frenzied animal with a gloved hand and yelling at the top of her voice. Kate and Edward were in their element, chasing the excited animal round and round the object of his excitement.

There was a strange expression appearing on Mr M's face as he reached down and touched the warm fur, matted and damp with spots of sea spray.

"Hello, little fellow, lost your way?"

Anna brushed down her skirt, which had received a shower of saltwater and winced with the overpowering seaweed smell. Her mood quickly restored as she beheld the strange saga unfolding before her. Within seconds the quivering, animal had climbed onto the checked blanket and snuggled into the welcoming arms, the pathetic whining giving way to a joyful yapping.

"Why, the animal is obviously crawling. Put him down, John, he could have contracted rabies," cried Anna her gloved hand covering her eyes in an attempt to blot out the scene. It was only as she turned to go that Mr M dutifully released the quivering beast and eased it reluctantly to the ground.

The children dancing alongside the retreating wheelchair were oblivious to their Aunt's concerns and intent only on making the acquaintance of the ensuing Spaniel, curious as to the unique fascination he held for their mysterious friend.

"Wait up, Boy," came the command.

The urgent voice floated in the air, like a distant hooter far out to sea, a nameless noise from a mysterious source. Kate was bringing up the rear and she came to a halt, turning she faced another more familiar stalker with a look of dismay and a questioning stare. It was the Munton girl, braced against the inclement weather, with only the flash of those roguish eyes visible in the gathering dusk, her shawl drawn tightly round her head and trunk. Just for a second Kate's heart went out to her. The grubby features, virtual rags, and below…. the bare, blotched toes.

"It's the Boy I'm a call-in, he brought the coppers an' me Ma's sent the remedy," she said arrogantly.

Kate stared hard at her incredulous assailant empathy fading, before finding a voice.

"Remedy?"

"The Valerian root….me' Ma swears by it."

So the deed had been done, Kate realised. The note duly served, the order delivered, and all of them none the wiser to Edward's absence. He must have slipped away as they reached the square, distracted as she was by the glitzy windows, the cheery mood of the adults and the hustle and bustle of the market place.

Before she had time to respond the 'go between' was there reaching up boldly for the package she proffered, a bashful grin lingering on his face. The girl caught obviously unawares, kept tight hold of the parcel, revelling in the sheer power she held over him, the roguish eyes alive with her moment of triumph before releasing it.

In seconds she had turned to go, streaking silently away, the flimsy form receding from view, melting before their eyes like a spectre in the fading light. Edward secreted the package in his breeches pocket, striding ahead of her without a word.

"You're dancing with the devil with that one, if you ask me," she hollered, quickening her pace.

It was only as Kate resumed her surveillance on the stairs that evening that her fears began to subside. It was quiet for that time of the evening, with a number of staff retired early in readiness for additional chores that went with the Christmas season. An intense light shone from the laundry room. It seemed Hicks was performing her usual nursing duties.

There was a gentle knocking sound and Kate looked up abruptly. Edward had appeared below, in his smart sailor suit and neatly cropped hair, illuminated by the strip of light that shone boldly from the little side room. For a moment there was only silence and then a mumbled response as the door swung open.

There was something distasteful about the scene being played before her and for the first time since his arrival Kate felt a distinct distance between her and her cousin. It was a void she couldn't quite fathom and a new and disturbing side to Edward's character was emerging. With the package delivered, Edward was gone leaving the corridor empty and the door wedged open.

From where Kate hovered on the staircase she could easily see the huge boiler that served the lower quarters of the house, the stone sink and draining board. And further into the interior the dubious duties of a disgruntled governess.

The chink of a china cup, a mist from a boiling saucepan and an odd odour Kate found quite repugnant. Duty complete Hicks loaded the tray with sugar and spoon, doubtless a subtle sweetener. She extinguished the light, lifted the tray and took the back stairs.

She thought of the Munton girl, her eagerness to earn a few pennies, her mother's knowledge of the hedgerows and her unlikely acquaintance with Edward.

Only a simple herb, used over the centuries to calm the mind, an inexpensive remedy, a mild sedative, a kind thought to ease someone's suffering. Hailed as a miracle cure by Mrs Munton and duly sanctioned by Dr Hinton.

What harm could there be in that?

Yet, what of the secrecy? The deception?

Kate wondered if she were worrying unduly about her cousin.

Just a passing phase perhaps; a reaction to his father's departure to the front or the absence of his mother?

These were questions that Kate juggled with in her head, questions that couldn't easily be answered.

CHAPTER 9. Kate's story – 1914

The change in the patient was as Dr Hinton remarked, 'extraordinary' and his praise for the Pickering household in shaping his recovery was voiced daily. His professional house calls were less frequent now but there wasn't a day went by when he didn't telephone to check on progress. The herbal tea which Mrs Munton had recommended, and which the doctor had sanctioned had indeed lifted his spirit and seemed to have all but vanquished the nightmares.

Another strange phenomena which appeared to be a vital part of his renewed health was the persistent attentions of his newly acquired four legged friend, who simply refused to disassociate with their bewildered guest. The mutual respect and the obvious pleasure they enjoyed was obvious to see and each one of them even Anna, looked forward to their walks each day. On their return from the beach the scruffy spaniel would mount the front steps only to be hastily shooed away by their Aunt. In seconds he could be found whining and scratching at the back door, where he remained for some hours, resolute in his determination to remain at Mr M's side.

By sundown Mrs Dawson was at her wits end with the mangy mutt, having doused him with the water several times, enticed him down the steps with tasty food scraps her patience was quickly wearing thin. At the end of the day it was Dorothy who acquired the task of tethering the animal securely in the stable block, dutifully responding to his pitiful howling that continued well into the night.

"So, where did this creature come from?" Charles was asking. "Must be from one of the local farms, shouldn't wonder."

It was a regular topic in the drawing room also, a pleasant distraction from the news on the front and an amusing anecdote for the children. Amazingly, Kate had noticed that the little dog was also a source of relaxation for Edward and as they played, laughing and running together, she could see him return to his former self.

Anna suddenly broke Kate's train of thought, bringing her back to the present.

"Can't seem to trace his owner, Mrs Andrews asked several times on her shopping trips but it's not a common breed roundabout …up on the moors perhaps, I'll get Lawrence to ask when he does his rounds."

Kate looked up at her father as he took his usual stance by the fireplace, her dream of being allowed to keep a puppy fading as he spoke.

"I'll ask at the club, there's a number chaps run pheasant shoots locally they may have one missing."

Edward was quick to respond, naïvely impulsive. He approached his uncle, standing boldly before him, dwarfed by the mountain of a man.

"He'd be no bother, Uncle Charles....I'd look after him," he offered, his upturned face glued to his guardian.

The look Kate gave her father prompted compassion, but it was short lived.

"Under no circumstances will that animal cross our threshold. It belongs in a stable block, it's a working animal - a tracker in the field."

Having aired his views Charles retired to his favourite chair and began flicking through the daily papers his mind now on more serious matters.

The silence that followed was punctuated only by a feeble cry that seemed to permeate through the building. A pathetic whimpering, largely ignored by the adult occupants each absorbed in their individual pursuits strangely unaware of the feeble bid for attention, which seemed only to attract the young.

It was Kate who reacted first. Eyes wide with alarm, her breath coming in short bursts she scanned the room for clues of compassion. Only Edward, his body trembling in readiness, glanced sullenly at the door and then at Kate.

It was a hasty retreat, their excuses barely noticed by the rest of the family who nodded and continued their more pressing activities.

Only when they were out in the corridor did they speak. Kate could hardly utter the words but Edward was there before her at the front door, slipping through the vestibule with urgency and flinging open the heavy door.

It seemed that someone was there before them. Perched on the topmost step, the checked blanket protectively hugging his legs and arms folded round the spaniel's shivering body. The whining had by now subsided together with the tension in his little body as he snuggled closer to his new companion. Mr M released his grip on the animal and turned abruptly as the door opened behind him.

"Oh, Edward....whatever is the rush. It's quite some time before our walk," the voice trembled a little.

His surprise at seeing them there was obvious. Lost in his own thoughts and painfully aware of the family's views and the recent discussions in the drawing room, running his hands through the lack lustre coat, a tentative tear appearing in the corner of his eye.

"He's alright, isn't he?"

Kate was beside them now, stroking the lively, white head and staring into the spirited eyes. For a moment they didn't speak, each fearing the worse and reluctant to voice it. The late morning sunshine did little to alleviate the chill wind coming off the North Sea and with neither of them dressed for a Whitby winter they huddled together for warmth.

"Do you know this dog, Mr M?" asked Kate.

"No Kate Pickering.....but he seems to know me."

Edward pulled back, staring hard and shaking his curly head.

"That's not possible Mr. M. There's no one for miles around who claims to know YOU."

"That's so Edward, and to tell the truth ....I don't even know myself, but this little feller' he knows me all right."

There were many questions on Kate's mind which suddenly spilled over.

"But where does he come from, Mr M and what are we going to do with him?" she implored.

With some discomfort and enormous effort the patient eased himself up, placed the pup on the threshold and walked gingerly down the front steps. He turned at the bottom and whistled a command, enticing the persistent pup to follow.

"You see Edward, he doesn't have any identification, no collar, no tag and so he and I we are alike, both lost in an alien world but maybe the two of us together, we can find ourselves."

It seemed it was not fitting for a domestic animal to use the front entrance, and so he was banished to the rear of the building. Secreted in the stable block on her Pa's instructions, fed and watered by Dorothy, he stayed. Just another unpaying guest without a name.

Now as the days sped rapidly toward Christmas the regular walks to the East bank became less frequent. Kate and Edward, lost in the euphoria of having a real pet spent most of their afternoons in the back yard, chasing the excitable pooch round and round whilst his new found master looked on. There was from time to time an inexplicable expression on the gentleman's face, his fingers working the tufts of the checked blanket nervously, as though trying to process his thoughts.

Around three in the afternoon when the studio was closed if the weather was fair, they would all set out. The sprightly Spaniel up front, the children in hot pursuit, with

Anna and Mr. M bringing up the rear. With the patient well on the mend, Hicks had renounced her duties, happy to hand over the escort duties to Anna. Kate relished her absence on these occasions, relieved to be with more amiable company and away from the disapproving looks.

Shuddering at the thought of the scheming that had gone on between Edward and the governess, the secrecy, the clandestine meetings she was thankful that the earlier rift between the two of them seemed to have healed. His recent interest in the playful pet, the enchanting stories of Alice in Wonderland and Mowgli in the Jungle that Mr M entertained them with had somehow brought about a change in him.

Today, he was in top form, full of youthful energy as he spun and whirled, skilfully guiding a wooden hoop with the beech wood stick and singing at the top of his voice, the eager Spaniel at his heel, barking in unison. After crossing the bridge they made their way through the streets, past the stone fronted shops and terraced cottages on their way to the pier. It was a favourite spot now, a place for reflection and a stirring of memories for Mr M. his recollections duly logged in the all essential diary.

They'd wrapped up warm with mufflers and gloves, the grey, menacing clouds chased by the bitter north wind, threatening a storm. As they approached the square Kate stopped, aware of an acute stillness that seemed to linger in the air. She scanned the street a little alarmed with a stark realisation that her cousin was missing. Not wanting to alert the adults she hastily retraced her steps, stopping at each shop front to peer in. It wasn't long before she saw him, his face taut and pasty, minute in the huge doorway of the Chemist store, a single chime from the brass bell above his head marking his presence.

Kate slipped into an adjacent alleyway, a hint of sadness in her eyes, uncertain of her cousin's purpose, concerned that this was another misguided mission. She sensed his uncertainty, the unease he displayed mixed with a dogged determination; an unmistakable trait of the Pickering character.

If only she could catch a glimpse of the crumpled paper in his hand that would without a doubt identify the agent, but her hopes were dashed as he wedged the hoop and stick firmly beneath his arm and slipped the crumpled paper into his pocket. He scanned the empty street before stepping outside.

It was now or never thought Kate. If she didn't tackle him straight away, heavens knows what trouble he could land himself in. It was one thing fetching a few harmless herbs to comfort a sick man but there was something underhand about sending a minor to collect preparations from the Chemist and Kate was intent on exposing the culprit. She stepped out from the shadows and confronted him.

“Edward…. There you are. I’ve been worried.”

Her cousin started, the hoop dislodging from the crook of his arm, and hitting the cobbled causeway with a thud.

“What business have you with the chemist?” she asked a little sternly, placing a firm hand on his shoulder.

Plainly startled by Kate’s appearance Edward dislodged the hand abruptly and made to retrieve the lost plaything, before marching ahead toward the square.

“Just tell me Edward… What have you in your pocket…..and who sent you?” she called after him.

The boy that turned to face her now, his eyes wide and innocent was physically familiar; the bandy little legs, the crisp linen sailor suit and wrinkled, woollen stockings. A typical nine year old, head full of nonsense, not yet clear on the boundaries of fact or fiction. He stood for a moment contemplating her, visibly reading her mind whilst trying to assemble his own.

“It’s a potion for Mrs Dawson,” he began. “It’s - it’s for the cockroaches in the kitchen!” he shouted. And then he was gone, tearing through the narrows streets clutching at the pocket of his woollen breeches where the paper parcel was concealed. Through the windswept square and out onto the pier, slipping back nonchalantly into his childhood world.

In spite of the chill afternoon they lingered there longer than planned, the spaniel as usual in playful mode and the children venturing onto the beach the sands now considered free of debris. Edward came to a halt at the water’s edge, his face peaked and glowing with the sharp winds, his dubious duties forgotten his eyes alight to sights and sounds of the shore. He whistled a welcome to the spirited spaniel, his boots retreating rapidly at the waves command as he skimmed a stone into the bubbling eddies. His face peaked and glowing with the sharp winds, he abandoned the cumbersome footwear. Breeches rolled to the knee, he raced along the shore leaping over rock pools with the eager pup in pursuit.

The Fisher folk were assembled there busy at their nets, undisturbed by the revellers their boats laying languid at the water’s edge, unmoved by the promise of a neap tide.

In his excitement, Edward had momentarily been unaware of their existence, the neat nimble fingers, curious tongue and vacant expressionless faces. He’d been oblivious to the change in the swell, the increasing roar of the ocean and the gathering of the clouds overhead. The light was fading quickly and Kate could hear Aunt Anna calling them from the pier, anxious that they should be gone.

It was almost three thirty and in less than an hour the sky would be as black as jet, with only the stars peeping through. There would be no guiding beam from the lighthouse nor welcome glow from the cottage windows for such were the constraints of war.

Kate was yelling too now, her voice rising on the wind, competing with the soaring gulls. But Edward wasn't listening, absorbed as he was in the delights of the shore. He'd even been oblivious to the stirrings of the young girl, the abandonment of her labours, bored with her chores and intent on causing mischief. Suddenly she was behind him taunting, teasing with a tap on his shoulder. She laughed high spiritedly, as he turned - shaken by her presence.

As Edward stumbled, losing his footing he spun round, liberating the crumpled note that had been secreted in his pocket. It fell conspicuously to the sands, soaking up the salty waters.

Kate's eyes widened.

What secret was written on that scrap of paper?

Which hand had written it?

Kate wished she'd hung onto him, made him turn out his pockets and hand over the toxic substance together with the handwritten note. But now it was too late.

Instantly the fisher girl took her opportunity, snatching up the paper and the contents it concealed, holding it aloft. The roguish eyes twinkled with glee as she turned on her heel, waving the coveted note aloft and inviting a chase. Now the sky became menacing, the sea a raging monster as the storm closed in. Rain fell like shards of ice, stabbing the leathery staunch features of the fishermen as they dashed for shelter, the women folk tripping behind them with their bags and chattels. Only Ma Munton remained, her eyes skimming the heavens, her voice filled with frustration.

"Eira - be away wiv' yer'. The light is fadin' and he's mighty angry up there."

Kate could only just hear the woman's words for the sound of the waves crashing on the breakers as she implored the girl to follow.

"Be warned mi' gal, there's nay much he does' ne see."

The rasping cry rang in Kate's ears, the sense of despair in the woman's voice touching her heart

"What business did the errant girl have with Edward?

"Why couldn't she just leave him be?"

The Spaniel yapping frantically at Edward's ankles, squealed and switched attention, the role of playmate turned protector. He stood between them his hackles raised, his body rigid and snarling at the tormentor.

Then the girl was gone, racing down the pier unperturbed by the worsening weather, with the boy in pursuit. Anna called in vain as Edward darted past and Mr M reached out trying unsuccessfully to harness the spaniel tearing after him like a whirlwind, yelping piteously. Nearby fishermen stopped on their journey home, shaking their weary heads and whispering a Hail Mary.

They watched on helplessly as the girl reached the end of the pier. She came to a sudden halt. Her ragamuffin garments now soaked, swathed her body like a mummies shroud, her hair unleashed to the mercy of the wind. Turning full circle she grinned gregariously, her breast rising and falling with the waves swell, the sun so low on the horizon now that her features were hard to define. Only the whites of her wild eyes pierced the shadows.

Edward stood motionless just steps away, golden curls flat against his forehead, face pleading and arms outstretched. He was only inches from the precious package, a single step and he would have it. He lunged forward.

Then suddenly she was upon the breakwater, balancing on tiptoe, pirouetting on the rim like a mystical water nymph, the angry swell rallying behind her, licking at her skirt hem, a warning of pending peril. But she paid no heed. Her face alight with the moment she beckoned to the small boy, waving the coveted note high in the air and willing him to follow.

"Edward…."came the collective cry from the shore.

And then in the blink of an eye she was gone, lost from view, sucked in by the sea. A scream went up from the beach, a strangled cry from the gathering gloom.

In an instant Mr M was on high alert, his ailing body switched to rescue mode he tore down the pier and leapt up onto the sea wall, scanning the surface a second before plunging into the violent foam. Kate watched in horror, her body unable to move, breath suspended, eyes wide as she took in the drama unfolding before her.

It seemed an cternity standing there as the storm took hold, muffling their cries, impinging on their prayers and putting the fear of God inside them.

And then the heads came bobbing, breaking the surface, the gasping for air followed by the cries of relief from the shore. Soaked to the skin but otherwise none the worse for her misadventure the wayward girl was plucked from the water and returned to her mother, her rescuer hailed a hero.

On the jetty Edward slipped his frozen hand in Kate's, a symbol of truce, a setting aside of differences, a new beginning. Gone was the crumpled paper, the vital evidence, the convicting seal. His childish face conveyed a certain sense of reprieve, safe and sound, his secret safe and the precious package still stowed in his soggy pocket.

The valiant rescue however took its toll on their heroic guest. His physical wounds not long healed and the persistent mental scars from those devastating nights when the sea threatened his destiny and death seemed inevitable. Whether the horrors of his experiences had surfaced again within him or his health had deteriorated once more following the unexpected soaking, they could not be sure. But on his return Mr M took to his bed, his nightmares returning, together with the fever.

Edward was also under the weather, confined to his room with a bout of influenza and despite their recent disagreements and the tension between them Kate had to admit she missed his endless questions and childish laughter.

The staff at number thirty two were again stretched to their limits, tending the sick, struggling to cope with the new rationing quotas, the everyday running of the household.

Kate blamed the crazy fisher girl for her part in all this. Her malevolent ways and her irrepressible charms that had captivated her cousin and put those she loved the most in imminent danger.

Kate could not eradicate Eira Munton from her mind. She wanted to protect Edward, to shield him from her influences, to banish her from the face of the earth. By night the girl seemed to haunt her every dream and in the daylight hours Kate was sure she had seen her familiar yet anomalous form weaving through the crowds on the West Cliff.

Life was considerably dull in the Pickering household of late and once lessons were over for the day Kate would make a beeline for the yard to find the faithful Spaniel. His lively welcome always cheered her and they would play long into the afternoon.

It was early one such evening as Kate was returning through the kitchen, that she stopped to ask Mrs Andrews if there were any scraps for the hungry hound.

"My, my, does that animal have an appetite.....why I only fed him this morning and yesterday he had a stack of mutton bones left over from the stew."

Kate knew that Mrs Andrews had a soft spot for the dog and that if it was at all possible she would outsmart Mrs Dawson with yet another trip to the larder.

"Well Miss Kate, I'll see what I can do but I can't promise. Why ye'll be takin' off our very plates before long to feed that mangy mutt."

It was warm and welcoming in the downstairs kitchen. There was a pleasant banter between the housemaids as they went about their chores, giggling and laughing and Kate lingered by the range taking in the tantalising smell of the lamb stew and watching Mrs Andrew's scurrying round her domain in her normal efficient manner.

"Well, child will that be all.....I'm running late as it is with extra visitors and all. Can I be getting you anything else?" she sighed, eyebrows raise in mock exasperation.

Kate shifted in her stockinged feet, suddenly self- conscious. Although she was always welcomed in the lower quarters of the house her presence was somewhat unusual at that time of the day.

She had a certain purpose in her presence there and as she cleared her throat she recalled her mother's visits to the kitchen, her imposing personality, her unique way of setting standards and organising her staff. One day maybe she would be standing there in her shoes, giving the instructions.

"Miss Kate…is there something else?"

There was something else of course and now Kate was brought back to the present with a jolt.

"The cockroaches.....have they gone now?" she mumbled.

For a second Mrs Andrews looked confused. She frowned, her pleasant demeanour quickly spent.

"The ones in the kitchen, Mrs Andrews. Have they gone?"

If Kate could have disappeared into the stone floor or vanished like a magician's rabbit she would surely have done so for the scream of alarm that came from the cook's lips was deafening.

"Why, young Miss.....there are no cockroaches in MY kitchen I can assure you of that. Whatever possessed you to ask such a thing?"

Kate felt her knees tremble and her stomach churn. She had never heard Mrs Andrews so angry before and hoped she would never hear her so again. Blushing profusely, her shoulders stiffened and, rescuing her boots from the side door, she scurried through the kitchen without a backward glance.

It was only when she reached the topmost step that she dared to stop, secure on the brink of no man's land betwixt floors where she felt safe again. Kate was aware that things were different below stairs, the things you said the way things were done. She only wanted to ease her mind, check that the goods had been delivered that the substance was in safe hands.

If there were no cockroaches in the kitchen then where was the substance now?

And what was it to be used for?

She pressed her head roughly against the bannister rail, willing the tears to come, wondering what Edward had done with the parcel. She rubbed her eyes, already red from the threatened tears, and tried to compose herself, desperately hoping that Mrs Andrews wouldn't raise the matter with her parents.

The lights were dim in the passageway and Kate could hear the grandfather clock chiming seven in the hallway above. There was movement on the upper landing and someone was closing the vestibule door. Distracted for a moment, so deep in thought Kate hadn't noticed the streak of light crossing the passageway below, emerging from the small laundry room. Since Mr M had been confined to bed again it was usual for him to eat of an evening in his room. Kate could distinctly hear the chink of crockery and the sound of running water as she usually did at this time. Young Dorothy appeared carrying a covered dinner plate and strode down the corridor to the illuminated laundry. She tapped on the door and walked in. A few harsh words were uttered before the housemaid rushed from the room, leaving the door wide open.

From where Kate sat in the shadows she could see the loaded tray. Steam rising from the elegant china plate as Hicks busied herself with the herbal tea - stirring the liquid to make the infusion. Then she disappeared into the depth of the room only to return with a matching saucer, a thin slice of lemon and a folded newspaper.

Kate looked over her shoulder. The dinner gong was sounding now and she knew she should be gone but something seemed to keep her there, fixed to the spot, wondering how her favourite visitor was today, how well he was recovering.

She glanced back to the kitchen as Hicks wedged the door open, her big articulate hands reaching down for the laden tray. Kate knew she couldn't wait a moment longer if she were to be punctual for dinner but somehow she found it impossible to tear herself away. Sitting there she could quite easily conjure up the memories, remembering the days they'd spent with Mr M, playing games and telling stories, chasing his memories.

She heard Hicks open the cupboard below. Kate knew she kept a store of biscuits secreted there which were kept for very special occasion. She reached inside her hand unsteady, then delved deeper. Very slowly she took out a paper packet and laid it on the work surface below. If not a biscuit, a little sugar maybe, to mask the bitterness, please the palette, help the patient unwind.

The package looked a little battered and with trembling hands Hicks took a spoon from the tray and slipped it inside the bag. Kate pressed her forehead firmly against the bannister, her eyes widening her mouth dropping open. The glow from the gas lamps gave ample light, enough to show clearly the fine grains as they slipped silently from the spoon into the steaming cup. Not the crystal cubes her mother lifted delicately from the sugar bowl with the silver tongs but a dubious looking grey substance the like of which Kate had never before seen.

A sharp tingle ran down Kate's spine, her hands gripping the staircase spindles in sudden panic as the full horror of what she was witnessing became clear. She held her breath not daring to move as the perpetrator dimmed the light, tucked the folded newspaper under her arm and set out for the back steps with the loaded tray.

It was only a minute paper packet, innocent in appearance, stored unnoticed in the capacious cupboards of the Pickering household and small enough to fit in a small boy's pocket.

CHAPTER 10. Lou's story – 2014

Lou stirred himself wearily. He flinched as a roguish spring thumped his lower rib as he shifted to find a more comfortable spot on the ageing chaise longue.

He was hardly in the best of moods. His whole body ached, head still vibrating with the Sisters of Mercy and his nostrils stung with the tenacious tang of last night's backie. He'd lain awake for what seemed like hours after the others had left. Light on alcohol, mind in a turmoil and his dreams fraught with flashbacks of the party. The image of Nette, bold and beautiful, framed in the doorway. So close he could virtually reach out and touch her, sensual, inspiring, the girl of his dreams. One minute there and the next gone, driven away in the dead of the night, just another failed relationship to add to his already bulging little black book.

A single shaft of light from the window caught his eye making him blink, yet another small aggravation to start the day. The screen flashed seven thirty. No good just lying there. Another few minutes and Merle would be down to create the perfect Latte and toast breakfast for her hunky hero.

He sighed, rescued the stray cushions from the threadbare carpet and eased himself up from the makeshift bed. He'd had enough of sleeping rough. Only one step up from those bedding down on the beach, huddled together by their driftwood fires with only a cold soup and tainted tobacco to sustain them. Gaz could well be out there with them now, he would put money on it, sharing their troubles, easing their minds offering whatever comfort he possibly could.

Then suddenly came a pang of guilt and he lifted the mobile and scanned the texts again.

"Hope everything OK with you and Ellie....thought you might have been home by now as no jobs on the horizon. Mum x"

She'd no need to worry now. They'd be packing their bags in a couple of hours, saying their goodbyes, checking the motor and heading for the open road. He responded with his usual lack of gratitude for her concern, "Hi Mum, back tomorrow, "and hung up.

He jostled with the retreating blankets, as directly on cue, Merle entered clad in last year's Rudolf onesie, red nosed and bleary eyed.

"Hi Lou....still not made it up with the darling Dag, then?" she teased.

It was the wrong moment and Merle sensed his irritation, making a bee line for the kitchen.

"Coffee, Lou?"

It was a pointless enquiry, falling on deaf ears as he continued to flick frantically through the texts.

"Everything alright?" Merle ventured after a short silence.

No….thought Lou it wasn't, but he didn't answer.

He'd had several texts along with his mother's. One from Aunt May giving an update on Butch, two from Retch when he'd been unable to contact Ellie and much to Lou's disappointment….there was nothing from Nette.

Then suddenly there was another text, flickering impatiently.

Could it be the crucial message he'd been waiting for?

The one that could change his plans yet again, make him stay just a little longer?

Probably just another message from Mum, he'd catch her later.

The screen flashed oddly, inexplicably, illuminating the room for just a second and Lou winced. No message just a photo…looked like a selfie but he certainly didn't recognise the young girl in the shot. Seemed like Ellie had been inviting the whole wide world to send selfies, not to mention the constant stream of images of his sister currently doing the Facebook circuits.

He glanced down again, trying to identify the young girl in the frame, but her face was unfamiliar. Long, chestnut locks, framing a pale, anxious face, eyes the deepest blue Lou had ever seen. She wasn't a Nette or a Susie or even a Jessabelle. No this was a younger girl, a minor, and as far as he could tell a complete stranger to him.

As if there weren't enough images of his sister currently touring the web it seemed like Ellie had been inviting the whole wide world to send her selfies. If only he could identify the girl, but he was completely baffled and for some uncanny reason the snapshot left him with a distinct feeling of unease.

"Penny for them…."

Lou grunted, picked up his makeshift bed and walked.

It was a typical winter morning, a ghostly mist swirling over the bay and icy winds to prompt warmer clothing. Lou was feeling the effects of kipping on the chaise longue, stiff neck, aching muscles and despite the benefits of the living room fireplace, he'd developed a nasty cold.

He pulled his collar up around his ears, clenched his teeth, braving the elements of a premature Whitby winter. It wouldn't be for much longer he told himself. One more night and then they'd be gone, back to civilisation, to the relative peace and quiet of Pudsey.

Turning the corner into the square, Lou felt a sharp gust of wind blow up from the sea, scattering a drift of fallen leaves that lay in his path and sending them spiralling through the air in a vibrant vortex. He walked briskly now, eager to be out of the icy blast that was irritating his sore throat and making his eyes water.

The inclement weather meant that the streets were mostly empty. But despite the gloomy morning the shop fronts were all brightly lit and welcoming. Lou stopped short before the little studio, took a deep breath and stepped inside. The familiar perfume beckoned him in, filling his senses and instantly lifting his mood. He anticipated the warm, sensitive voice and that melting feeling she gave him inside.

It wasn't the greeting he'd expected and although he had already anticipated a frosty reception ……he hadn't been prepared for this.

"Can I help you?"

A second passed before he realised that the woman behind the counter was not Nette. She spoke the words efficiently, automatically, addressing her customer with the utmost courtesy. Lou smiled disenchanted by the unfamiliar voice and peering into the depths of the store in hope of other occupants.

"Oh, I was looking for Annette," he blurted.

The smartly dressed female came forward briskly, studying his face with a certain curiosity mixed with the mere hint of disapproval. Lou noted the salt and pepper hair, tied neatly behind her head and the pale blue enquiring eyes that seemed to hold a certain sadness. An uneasy silence ensued.

"You've just this second missed her, won't be back today……she's an appointment at the hairdresser."

Lou could tell just by the tone of her voice, the sharp response and way she instantly turned her attentions back to the stock taking that the conversation was destined to end. On impulse he strode the few paces to the counter, his hopes dashed but not ready to be given up on, not just yet.

"Hairdresser?" he echoed. Lou wasn't familiar with hairdressing salons, certainly not the ones round here.

"It's up on Henrietta Street, not too far," came the indifferent response from the unrelenting back view.

She can't have got too far, Lou thought. The intense rush of fragrance as he stepped through the door told him she wasn't long gone. Instantly he was on the square, retracing his steps, braving the inclement weather, ignoring the inflamed throat and dull headache.

In the distance Church bells signalled the end of the Sunday service, as congregation mingled with shoppers in the narrow street. Usually jam-packed with tourists the higgledy-piggledy thoroughfares were quiet now, devoid of the demonic revellers and mid-week shoppers. Retailers rejoiced in the winter opening times and Lou was grateful for the ease of movement as he slipped into Henrietta Street. He stopped, scanning the pavements, the people, signboards anything that might give him a clue to her whereabouts. Time was not on his side and his luck was rapidly running out.

And then he saw her....just a transitory glance, the fleeing angel, slipping into the opposite alleyway oblivious to her pursuer. Dressed in a pale pink boucle jacket and black laced boots, the matching bag swinging from her shoulder.

He would have cried out but he knew it was pointless, out of earshot she was lost in a world of glitz and glamour, a haze of hairspray and pending panache.

The church goers were in full flow now, having descended the hundred and ninety nine steps, they clustered in shop doorways, blocking the pavements, delivering their spirit of goodwill to all. Lou made polite excuses as he writhed his way through the throng and, on reaching the alleyway, he was acutely aware that he was leaving the shops behind. Nette disappeared around another corner leading into a network of little passages and he quickened his pace.

"Nette....."

His voice bounced from wall to wall, echoing eerily into the narrow passageway. It was only a short distance to the corner and Lou covered it, in less than a second.

"Nette" he whispered, breath escaping cloudlike in the clammy air.

Then she was there, looking at him intensely with those deep blue eyes, her face flushed with the first hint of winter. It was difficult to read what was going through her mind but Lou looked deeper into her very soul.

"You've every right to........." he began.

"No Lou, please don't, I can't talk now," she said, her eyes burning into his face.

This couldn't happen, he thought….she can't just walk away.

"I really don't deserve……" she began to speak and then froze.

The angel that stood in the dim alleyway, her face harsh and inflexible shook her head slowly and turned away. Lou could still see the shining aura above her head, the sincerity in her voice, her unquestionable beauty and the growing distance between them.

She began to walk swiftly, silently, only her heels sounding the retreat, gripping the shoulder bag with a resolute passion. Lou followed, afraid to let her go, afraid to give up, to admit defeat.

"You can't just walk away, I need you Nette……"

The lack of response was crushing and Lou suddenly had the feeling he'd miscalculated, misread the signs, and completely imagined the whole chemistry between them. Surely not.

He quickened his pace in line with Nette's, snaking the dimly lit alleyways, devoid of sunlight, endorsing his mood.

"I just need to tell you, because I'm leaving………. going home," he ventured.

His revelation didn't prompt a response and Nette kept going, breaking out onto another thoroughfare lined with higgledy, piggledy cottages, with clear views out to sea across the terracotta roofs. There were no shops here no working salons touting for custom on a Sunday.

"Nette"

And now Lou realised it was his last chance, his final moment.

"Nette…don't go…….. I love you!"

There, it was said. He'd bottled it up inside, afraid to say it even, utter his true feelings, and now he waited, dreading the response.

For a second she paused again, deep in thought perhaps, playing the words over in her mind like a treasured track. Lou waited.

Surely he'd made some lasting impression? Or was it just a holiday romance, a fleeting moment of passion or a brief but unremarkable affair?

“The weather’s lousy, Ellie needs to get back to that low life,” he continued in full swing. “I can’t stand the B and B any longer, it’s a bloody nightmare and besides there are no jobs at ……….”

Before he could finish his spiel Nette turned abruptly, the true blue eyes charged with a ferocity he’d never seen before. The hostile tone that she adopted came as a shock and Lou recoiled, stepping backwards into the gloom.

“It’s all about you Lou….isn’t it? You have no idea. You live in your own little world, full of restrictions, where no one understands you. You’re a martyr, a slave, a reluctant chaperone, and when you speak everyone has to listen……

She stood to face him now, full on, in fighting mode, acute aggression clouding the angelic face. Clutching the shoulder bag like a veritable life support. Then she continued.

“You never once asked about me, Lou,” she stammered. “My family, my friends, my hopes and dreams….not once Lou Bannister.”

“You never think of anyone but yourself,” she said raising her voice to screaming pitch as she turned to face him.

Then she turned to go. He really had blown it this time and yes…..it was all his fault.

Lou watched her sprint onto Church Street, his head reeling from her words. She was right of course, he was self- centred, egotistical and full of self- pity. And true, he knew nothing of her life.

She quickened her step, slipping through hidden passageways he never knew existed. Following at a pace his heart racing, he called out again as she mounted the church steps, two at a time without looking back. As she reached the stone seat at the top, the light was beginning to fade and in seconds Lou was beside her, catching his breath.

Standing motionless by the old yew tree, he stood defeated, filling his lungs with the salt sea air.

In a moment she had spun round, hair blowing in the blustery wind, a very different expression on the lovely face. Squinting in the fading light, Lou stood back, trying to get a full measure of her mood. There was a softness there he hadn’t seen a moment ago and for a second he could sense the connection, relive thc past, the strong bond that once united them.

Suddenly her face crumbled, her eyes shimmered with promised tears, her arms hanging limply at her side. In seconds she'd stumbled toward him, sobbing helplessly as he pulled her into his arms.

"Whatever is the matter?" he mumbled.

She stood at arms- length and reached out to touch his cheek gently, forcing a weak smile through the tears. Taking his hand in hers she walked, telling him her story as the emotion flowed. The details of which were imprinted on his brain and saturated his very soul.

ANNETTE MC BRIDE and her elder brother, Ian had been brought up in Whitby by two devoted and loving parents, Paul and Sylvia. Her father ran his own shipping company, her mother was a director at the firm. And her brother soon followed his father's footsteps, becoming a partner. Annette was bright and beautiful, she was a popular girl and having passed her exams with flying colours she took a place at the local Grammar School.

Then her mother fell ill. The doctors said it was a malignant tumour, and that there was no hope. It spread through her like wild fire within just a few months of being diagnosed with the Cancer.

Annette was thirteen years old when her mother died and from that moment her life would never be the same. Plucked from an idyllic childhood and plunged into profound grief she found herself failing at school and socially excluded.

She shunned her friends dreading, their well-meaning sympathy, their constant questions, the whispering in the corridors. Unable to come to terms with her grief and move on with her life she withdrew into a world of her own.

Her father facing a lifetime without the only woman he'd ever loved, went to pieces. He took to wandering off for days on end and finally disappeared without a trace, leaving his son and daughter to fend for themselves.

When Ian left for University in Lincoln, Annette moved in with her aunt and uncle, Sally and Mike. They were kindly and supportive but failed to reach her in her grief or to fill the terrible void left in her life.

There was no explanation of her father's departure, nor did he leave a forwarding address.

Paul Mc Bride had vanished off the face of the earth, abandoning family, friends and his thriving business unable to face the pain of looking at his precious daughter the one who reminded him so much of his adored wife.

As their eyes met briefly over the vast four poster, Lou realised he was seeing Nette for the very first time. The real Nette. He knew her most intimate secrets, her wildest dreams and even her hopes for the future.

She stood before him, unclothed and uncomplicated.......an open book with a succession of sequels. Now he felt he could literally step inside, rework the text, and alter the outcome, a protagonist with purpose, a hero with a cause. He'd change the plot, numb the pain and deliver a happy ending.

The space between them that had recently felt like a great chasm was rapidly closing. He had infiltrated her mind, entered her very soul and now he was ready to explore her body.

As he pulled her closer, bridging the gap a little further he could feel the smoothness of her skin rubbing against him, the sweetness of her breath, the heady perfume filling his head. She responded passionately, taking the lead, spurring him on, breaking down the barriers that had kept them apart for so long.

Slipping his hand round the curve of her back he sought the lips he thought he would never kiss again and sweeping her onto the four poster, he eased into her.

The dawn was breaking as Lou made his way back to the B and B leaving the grandeur of the West Cliff behind him, his mind and body still replaying the events of the previous night. It wasn't the grandness of the guesthouse, the comfort of the bed or even the ambience of the dimly lit room that made the night so memorable. Right now he couldn't think of anything else, nor would he want to.

It was chilly in the early morning, but the wind had dropped and the slither of the sunrise lining the bay suggested an improvement in the weather. As he crossed the bridge and looked out over the harbour he realised that life wasn't really so bad. Things were actually looking up and nothing and no one could bring him down again. After all he'd a lot to be thankful for.

Yes, his parents were busy people, but at least they came home most nights, he and Ellie had a permanent roof over their heads and there was always food on the table. It was time he started to count his blessings and realise just how fortunate he was in life.

He paused on the corner, a ringtone indicating a text on his mobile. It was Nette. He smiled, reliving the past few hours once more. He'd talk to Ellie and get back to her. His plans to up sticks and leave didn't seem so urgent now. He stood upright, brushing the hair from his bleary eyes and set off again along the road.

Life was great, couldn't get any better now that Nette was back in his life.

As he neared the B and B he became aware of a huge black estate car parked at an angle across the road.

"Thoughtless prat," Lou said out loud. "Can't anyone park straight these days?"

Moving closer he approached the back window. The registration didn't ring a bell, must be one of the neighbours Lou thought. The windscreen was steamed up and he bent to take a look inside. It seemed the driver was still in there.

"Holy Cow, mate," he said, banging on the roof. "Can't you read? ….No parking at any time!"

When there was no response Lou moved to the front and began hammering on the passenger side window. The gap at the top was barely wide enough for Lou to slip his fingers in and the glass reluctant to shift, its surface cloud and it wouldn't budge.

Then he realised the headlight were on full beam and shining directly into the front room of the B and B. Lou went to open the door but found it locked.

"For Christ's sake," he muttered under his breath as he reached the front.

He took a step backward. The driver was asleep at the wheel and judging by the expression on his face, the gaping mouth, the overwhelming stench of alcohol he was probably in no fit state to drive. Worse than that it was a face he knew all too well. Then Lou lost it.

"Retch…….You bloody idiot," he moved in again, shouting and hammering on the window. Gaining no response he threw himself against the car and tried rocking it. Instantly the occupant lurched forward, slumping over the steering wheel, the full weight of his body activating the hazard lights and alarm on the dashboard.

Suddenly all hell was let loose, windows opened above and people started screaming some running out into the street, clutching their hands to their ears to blot out the noise. Lou pushed past the startled onlookers and into the B and B. By the time he'd managed to find a hammer and smash the window to gain entry it was too late ……..It was less than fifteen minutes before the police and ambulance arrived, but the death knell for Richard Etchington had likely sounded some considerable time before.

A frantic Ellie wept beside the car, clutching the bereaved Minor bird she'd prised from his master's shoulder, dazed and disoriented but still chattering loudly.

"Rum and Black…,"it squawked. "Gin and Tonic" "Sex on the Beach."

At six am they pronounced Richard Etchington dead at the scene and following the post-mortem, a full criminal enquiry was launched.

CHAPTER 11. Kate's story – 1914

She heard the kitchen door click and slunk back into the shadow of the stairwell, hardly daring to breath. The approach of their menacing mentor always set her heart thumping. The challenge of making the grade in the schoolroom, only speaking when spoken to, obeying the rules was a small price to pay for the continuing approval of her dear Papa and a simple show of willingness to make something of herself.

Kate held on to the thought as she heard the footfall on course for the little laundry room, the creaking hinges and then the flare of the gas light. She said a silent prayer, crossed her fingers and hoped she was mistaken. The door was fully open tonight, the lamps flooding the passageway with a golden light. Inside the evening activity continued, the chink of a cup, the hiss of the urn with the obnoxious aroma of Valerian root tainting the air. It caught in her throat, making her gag.

Who wouldn't need a sprinkling of `sugar' to please the palette, to dull the obnoxious after taste?

Sitting cross legged in her favourite spot on the uppermost step was somehow not so pleasurable now. Her heart beat louder than she had ever heard it before as she watched a replay of the deadly scenario.

Her hands tense and clammy she gripped the spindles, hoping upon hope that she'd got it wrong, misread the signs and that it was all a figment of her imagination.

She had to think carefully, gather evidence, bide her time, for clearly, who would believe a twelve year old girl?

Yet, time was running out, one more dose and the effects could be irreversible and then it would be too late.

There was talk of the front in the dining room this evening, tainting the thrill of the coming season and the delights of the evening meal. Papa talked of conditions in the trenches, the lack of supplies and aired his doubts about the war being over by Christmas. As usual the conversation was edited, modified for the ears of a minor and Kate remained quiet, thankful at least that, unlike Edward, she wasn't missing her father. Charles had served in the Boer War, been commended for his outstanding service, but the shrapnel that lodged itself in his thigh had caused permanent damage. His duties now restricted to tending survivors of the storm and the war wounded.

Kate knew she should speak to her father, tell him of her suspicions. But this wasn't the right moment, and besides it would be pointless as she couldn't provide the proof it would take to convince him. She sat at the table deep in thought oblivious to the ongoing conversation, her mind focussed on events of the past few days, reliving her night watches, the unspeakable scenario that had unfolded before her very eyes. Her only consolation lay in the knowledge that Edward was safely away from the governess's influence, tucked away in his little bed, he was making a good recovery.

"Kate.....your soup is getting cold," said her mother. "Do hurry, dear. Dorothy is waiting to serve the main course."

It was unusual to see their young maid in the dining room, her duties normally restricted to the kitchen. Kate looked up at the drained face, the unruly hair, the crumpled apron, hands hovering impatiently over the china bowl. The growing number of visitors in the house meant additional work, longer hours and all for the same pay. The days when Dorothy lingered in the hallway to recite nursery rhymes, pick up a toy soldier or mend a broken doll were long gone. Kate couldn't remember the last time she'd even seen her smile.

With the remainder of the dishes cleared the young maid returned to the kitchen and the discourse resumed. There was talk of the hardship and plight of soldiers, and how the Red Cross were meeting on Mondays to dispatch parcels bound for the front. Anna had been collecting wool scraps from the local mills and was rallying an army of local women to knit socks for squaddies and Papa had been fortunate to receive a most welcome consignment of tobacco and cigarettes for their war wounded.

"Every little helps of course," he was saying. "And even more important they've agreed additional supplies for the men at the front."

Kate thought about Edward's father out there devoid of human comforts, open to the raw elements and fearing for his life, with few comforts and a heavy heart. There wasn't a day went by when Kate didn't think of the serving soldiers, praying for their survival and safe return. She prayed for all the war wounded who lodged at No 32 and most of all for Mr M whose life once again was held in the balance.

United in their individual war efforts, the Pickering family spirits were lifted momentarily as Charles roared with laughter at the cartoons in The Times depicting smiling squaddies receiving their precious parcels from home.

Suddenly the frivolity ceased as the door opened abruptly and a rather agitated Dr Hinton appeared, standing motionless on the threshold.

"Lawrence, my boy.....you're a little late for dinner, is there something wrong?"

Kate always warmed to Dr Hinton, his friendly face and gentle manner but today it was obvious something was troubling him. He came into the room, slowly shaking his head without speaking.

“Well, man?” Papa ventured, indicating a spare seat at the table.

Everyone’s attention was with him now, pivoting round to see their visitor.

“I called in on our mystery gentleman…he’s had a rough time it’s true but he should be making progress now. The dousing last week set him back I know but he’s failing again and I just can’t understand it.”

He clutched the back of Anna’s chair, a baffled expression flashing over his face as he looked enquiringly over at Papa. Kate had not seen Mr M for a couple of days due to the return of his fever and Hicks had been most forceful in her orders that he should not, under any circumstances be disturbed.

“He’s complaining of headaches - the confusion has returned and all his strength has gone.”

Anna always had a soothing word for her brother in law. The loss of David had affected him acutely, his ensuing grief somehow reflected vigorously in the additional care he showed his patients.

She turned to face him. “I saw him only yesterday and in truth I thought he was improving.”

“Yes….I believed so myself. Even with the soaking he got, I never expected this…..”

There was a break in his voice, Kate noted and a certain sadness in the tone as he turned to go.

“I’ll call in first thing tomorrow. I’ve changed his medication and asked Hicks to stay with him throughout the night.”

Kate cringed at the mere mention of the name. And now Dr Hinton had asked her to nurse him night and day. She wanted to scream out, stop him in his tracks, and persuade him to let someone else watch over him. But somehow the words wouldn’t come and she sat there as though her little body was riveted to the chair. She bit her tongue, knowing to speak up now would be futile.

“Right Man, I’ll discuss it with Hicks. She’ll be more than willing and she knows his routine. “

Kate squirmed. She knew his routine alright and indeed the everyday habits of the rest of the household. All part of her cunning scheme to manage every aspect of the patient’s care and carry out her evil plan.

It was true that her father put Maria Hick's on a pedestal, trusted her implicitly and afforded her the utmost respect when it came to his children's care and education. After all hadn't they surpassed all his expectations, his highest hopes and now Florence had won a scholarship to Wimbledon House, the much acclaimed girls school.

It was mother's hope that someday Florence would even take on a doctorate at Cambridge. She talked of changes for women generally, the efforts of the suffragettes, and the right of freedom of speech for all. The war had opened up new opportunities for the fairer sex and Mama who was a great supporter of women's rights used every bone in her body to support the cause.

Acutely aware of her inability to do anything to change the evening's course of events, Kate remained silent.

"Yes, Lawrence," her mother continued. "I intended to look in on Mr. M yesterday but it was so late after the Red Cross meeting."

Kate knew her mother visited their patients regularly, usually on a daily basis and even when she was engrossed in her charity work her thoughts were always with the sick and injured in their care.

It was her Aunt that spoke next as she crossed the room and put a calming hand on her mother's shoulder.

In times of trouble Aunt Anna was always there, offering advice and support even through her own recent troubles. Kate loved her intensely, trusted her implicitly and treasured the times they spent together. Furthermore, she could rely on her utmost discretion when dealing with sensitive matters.

"Don't worry yourself, Esther…..I will go to him and I can pass on Lawrence's instructions at the same time."

Kate had to think quickly, she couldn't let this continue a second longer. She glanced around the room, taking in the anxious faces, knowing there was only one person she could truly confide in, and that was Aunt Anna.

The timing was of course perfect and the scenario repeated with careful precision. Kate had induced her Aunt to join her on the topmost step, although not without a certain alarm at her niece's covert activities and still unsure what was actually troubling her. They huddled together betwixt floors listening to the activity in the little laundry room below, their faces taut with expectation.

As before the door stood ajar and the sinister sequence was replayed before their eyes. Kate watched as her Aunt struggled to understand exactly what she was witnessing. Her brow furrowed, testing the softness of her flawless skin, her lips taut and a bewildered look in her eye she watched the grey granules float effortlessly into the china cup, duly stirred by an efficient hand.

She looked at her niece questioningly, shaking her head and then returned her gaze to the lighted room as the governess made her way determinedly along the corridor with the loaded tray.

It wasn't totally fitting, Kate thought as they entered the six by eight room, for them to appear downstairs unannounced nor was it usual for them to peer into Mrs Dawson's clean and ordered cupboards. But this wasn't any usual occurrence in the Pickering household and it was of the utmost importance that her family were fully aware of the deadly secret hidden within its walls.

Her Aunt was almost six foot tall in her stocking feet and could easily reach into the farthest recess of the laundry room cupboard to discover the crumpled paper packet and classify the content. It didn't take long for them to read the chemist's label, complete with instructions for eradicating the most persistent of household pests.

Kate gripped her Aunt's hand firmly and checking the corridor, she retraced her steps, mounting the stairs she steered them through the shadows for fear of being seen. Now she needed to convince her Aunt that far from keeping any imaginary cockroach population in check the substance was indeed destined for an entirely different victim.

The door of the drawing room was closed and Kate had been standing in the grand hallway for some time now, her heart beating rapidly in anticipation of the ensuing discussion. Her aunt would of course handle this rationally, with her usual sensitivity and with a calm assertiveness that never failed to gain her father's attention. It was eerily quiet, with a lack of the after dinner dialogue that generally permeated the Pickering household. All Kate could hear was the distant yelping of the stalwart spaniel, which muffled Aunt Anna's trembling voice within.

She was suddenly aware of a footfall behind her and slipping behind the nearby hall robe, she held her breath. Someone approached the drawing room with a tray. It was usual at this time for the family to take cocoa before retiring and this evening was no exception. Kate could just make out the lean figure, hesitating in the darkness before the doorway, balancing the loaded tray in one hand she tapped tentatively.

It was a few seconds before the response was heard.

"Come..."

As Dorothy entered the room she faltered, perhaps aware of the tense atmosphere, the unwelcoming reception. She stepped forward with an apology, placing the tray on a side table and made the obligatory curtsy before serving the steaming cups.

"I take it you wish to sit with him yourself then, Anna," Papa continued, returning to his armchair. "I'll have Mrs Dawson bring some refreshment up for you before she retires."

"Thank you, Charles."

Kate crept from behind the hall robe edging her way toward the open door. She didn't want to be seen but her curiosity propelled her forward to where she had a clear view of the company. Aunt Anna stood with her back to her, message delivered, seemingly ready for retreat. Her shoulders relaxed, no doubt encouraged by the sign of her brother's understanding and imminent support.

"I do think we are wise to take the precaution, Charles," she spoke in a whisper, glancing over at the conscientious housemaid. "Therefore I shall speak with Hicks, before I go up."

The words had hardly left her lips when a very, anxious and animated Edward appeared in the doorway, his chest rising and falling with the effort of running, his cheeks flushed a fiery crimson. Standing behind him now, Kate could hardly believe her ears as he began to speak.

"You've got it all wrong, Uncle Charles……….it's not Hick's, she's NOT to blame," he screamed at the top of his voice.

Stopping in his tracks, his breath came in short spurts as he scanned the little gathering. Kate had never heard Edward speak out like this, challenge his elders, air his beliefs. From where she was standing, he looked so insignificant there, his fragile frame enveloped in the overlarge nightshirt, his bare feet braving the chill of the parquet flooring.

Then distracted by the clatter of tea cups, his eyes flashed in the direction of the other occupant.

"It's not Hicks……….it's not the one with the evil eye, it's HER."

A single china cup slipped silently from the maid's grasp, striking the parquet with a resounding clatter and smashing into a million pieces.

CHAPTER 12. Lou's story – 2014

Huge snowflakes floated silently from an ivory sky as the cortege wound its way along the harbour front, turning effortlessly onto Green Lane. There was a calmness that always came with the first snowfall, like a flannel on a fevered brow, a soothing song, the comfort blanket for a crying child. In the stillness of a winter morning, fingers numb and hearts heavy the little band huddled together in the back of the shiny black limousine, bound for the ancient chapel of St Mary's. Lou, Nette and Ellie crushed in the back of the second vehicle with their grim faced guru Kalen, a fitting front man.

It was odd to gaze on those familiar faces that on a normal day held all the trappings of tragedy. The pale ghostlike features, bloodshot eyes the very traits that set the Goth community apart. And yet, curiously today they mingled with the mourners, undetected, unremarkable, a suitable mask for a melancholy day.

Following the hearse - the lead car had been reserved for Richard's family - were his parents and two elder brothers who'd arrived that morning to stay with relatives in Whitby. They were obviously finding it hard to come to terms with their son's untimely death, trying to piece together the events of his last hours, his final movements. And now the results of the post mortem had revealed another, more sinister side to his life. That of a hardened drug addict.

For Lou this of course had a more frightening aspect, an unvoiced dread that in some way Ellie had been involved. Maybe not as a user, he was pretty sure of that but certainly as a conscious accomplice to an illegal practice. He couldn't even look at her, speak the words but both of them knew she had a lot of explaining to do.

Lou's only solace was that Nette was there by his side, supporting him as ever, mindless of her own life struggles, her arm wedged firmly round his waist, the warmth of her body a constant comfort.

It was a simple service with a sombre faced minister, two unfamiliar hymns and a few lines from the scriptures. A strange programme for a modern day funeral, Lou thought. There was a distinct lack of uniqueness about the whole event and marked shortage of sentiment, as they lowered his body into the earth with only the silent tears of his sister to mark the occasion.

"Thanks for being here," Lou was saying as they left the graveside. "Don't think I could have managed it without you."

"It's not a problem Lou…and somehow I've always felt at ease here in the churchyard."

The snow was easing now leaving the stone flags beneath their feet passable. The storm clouds were retreating rapidly. Above their heads a watery sunshine peeped through. Nette stepped out onto the path, her face glowing and calm.

"It's not a problem Lou.....and somehow I feel at ease here in the churchyard." she said.

As they began to walk toward the waiting cars, Nette suddenly stopped and unlinked her arm. She walked a few paces and beckoned Lou to follow. The little side path was overgrown with a persistent bindweed that crunched beneath their feet but protected from the elements by a crumbling stone wall clothed in mildewed ivy. Lou followed, welcoming a break from the wild, open churchyard and a moment's relief from the gloomy proceedings.

They came to a standstill by an unremarkable plot, a spray of yellow roses interspersed with baby's breath, the only attractive feature.

"It's not a lavish stone. Dad was never ostentatious. He kept it simple.... unlike the rest of the Mc Bride stock. You can't gild a lily, he used to tell Mum."

Lou frowned, playing the words over again in his head. Watching the deep blue eyes, overflowing with emotion, he focussed on the plain headstone with an endearing inscription marking the resting place of Sylvia Anne Mc Bride.

"She was beautiful and she had so much to live for," Nette was saying "I miss her so much."

They sat on the little wall for a time as Nette talked about her parents. How happy they had been and how they'd worked together to build the family shipping business. Lou suddenly realised that Nette had never spoken to anyone about her mother before, the pain of losing her, the enduring emptiness inside.

"I dreaded anyone asking about my family. Talking about the ordinary, everyday things that everyone took for granted. And then to actually say the words 'my mother is dead'. I couldn't talk to Aunt Sally or Uncle Mike because they were grieving too and then when my Dad disappeared.....it seemed like neither of them had ever existed."

The eyes said it all, beautiful and bewitching yet somehow today, unusually humourless. The anguish and loneliness suddenly rekindled in the melancholy of a midwinter day.

"And your father?" Lou said softly, sensing the acute pain.

Nette sighed and looked away, her breath rising, effortlessly in the air, like a fleeing phantom. It was a few moments before she spoke.

"He moved to Scarborough, I believe. Last we heard he was living with a young woman, a clairvoyant by all accounts; a seafront soothsayer, a fortune teller."

It was Lou's turn to comfort Nette now, taking her cold hands in his he took off his jacket and wrapped it round her trembling shoulders, pulling her close. He knew then how thoughtless he'd been, how blind and selfish about his own life. Taking his own parents for granted, always assessing them, criticising them. He'd never thought of the hours they'd worked, just to keep them afloat, always away from the family home, no bedtime stories or school concerts, missing all those precious days of their childhood.

Nette eased herself slowly from the clinch, returning to the little grave she rearranged the yellow roses and ran a reflective hand over the gold lettering of the simple headstone.

"This is all I have left, Lou."

She sighed, brushed down her skirt and turned to go.

They bypassed the waiting car and made their way out onto the allotments, through the bramble hedge and then down the winding streets to the harbour side. Away from the tourist gaze and the remaining mourners. There would be time enough for the necessary condolences, idle reminiscences and the crocodile tears when they returned to the B and B. And for now he just needed to be with Nette.

Somehow the telling of Nette's story had given him a new outlook on life, and their relationship had given him a new direction in life, a fresh start.

They walked steadily, the ground mushy beneath their feet and a chill wind penetrating the late morning sunshine. By the time they reached the bridge, the traffic was almost at a standstill, pedestrians negotiating the clearer parts of the pavement, the worsening weather as usual bringing the town to a standstill.

Lou was trying desperately to ignore the mobile reverberating in his pocket from time to time. He lost count of the times Ellie's selfies had appeared on his screen recently and if things had been different, he would have simply turned the power off. Perdy had gladly taken on the temporary role of chaperone, a compassionate friend, a willing support but this was his only link and a vital one.

"Everything OK?" Nette was asking.

Lou smiled, suspended in a hollow between the two most important females in his life. He retrieved the phone clicked onto texts to check on updates and shook his head as the crazy photo appeared again.

"I know she's in a state of shock....but why all the cute photos? It doesn't make any sense."

"Oh God...it's there again!" Lou snapped. "I wish she'd stop linking me in, it's getting quite annoying now."

"Let me see, Lou," Nette leaned over his shoulder, to get a better view.

A strange and peaceful look crossed her face then, lighting up the gloom of a winter day and making him smile.

"You certainly are a mystery, Annette ......What are you thinking about?"

"Oh, nothing really. Come on, Lou, if you really want to walk me home, let's go. I promised Aunt Sally I'd be at the studio for one o'clock."

Standing there on the West Cliff, Lou scanned the shore. He'd never imagined that Nette could live here, just a stone's throw from the humble environs of the opposite shore, with its crowd of humble cottages and labyrinth of shopping streets. In all his many visits to Whitby Lou had never really considered the contrasts. But now he gazed in awe at the splendour of this part of the coastline, the huge cliffs, the bracing wind from the sea and the magnificent buildings that lined he promenade.

"You have a house here?" Lou was saying, as he awoke from his reverie.

They moved toward the nearby whalebone arch, which Lou had seen so many times from the opposite shore and then turned about, gazing across at the splendour of number thirty two.

"Well, it's an apartment really. On the second floor. It's my Aunt and Uncle's. We lived in the basement when....when Mum was with us," Nette stopped, the words teetering on her tongue, reluctant to leave.

"When we were all together," she finished.

Lou couldn't afford the huge hotels that lined the seafront, just one night in the plush guest house had left him skint. He grimaced as he thought about the B and B, its grimy windows and perilous porch, the cracked mirror and cobweb curtains. How gross compared with the splendour here.

"Number 32. It's been in our family from way back, three, four generations even and in the early days, during the Great War they opened it up for a temporary hospital."

The four storey block, built in traditional Georgian style, fronted the esplanade, its windows looking directly out onto the bay. Its grand facade was something Lou had only ever seen on the cover of glossy magazines. And now, he was grappling with the idea that Nette, could actually live here, part of a separate set, an elite society and quite possibly a woman of some means.

Lou jumped as his phone vibrated again, the ring tone indicating the return of the familiar photo. He fumbled in his pocket.

“Damn it!” he snapped.

Nette smiled again as she moved toward him. She shook her head and gave him a perfunctory peck on the cheek.

“Have to go, dreamboat....but call in at the studio if you get time this aft. I’ve something I want to show you.”

Instantly she was gone, leaving Lou to continue with his conjectures. He waved as she reached the far pavement, his feet reluctant to shift but his mind on the dubious delights of the forthcoming wake.

The afternoon that followed, Lou could have easily predicted. After all it was in most respects no different to any other funeral, except that, in this instance, it had been totally unforeseen, a shocking end to a young life, and with many questions left unanswered. Richard’s parents were still reeling from the shock of the autopsy. The document revealed a massive 190mg of Cocaine in his bloodstream together with an undisclosed volume of alcohol. Which in turn produced a toxic chemical known as Coca ethylene, providing the fatal dose.

Returning to the B and B Lou walked in on an eerie silence, broken only by the squawking of the insistent mynah bird. Still in full swing with his raucous requiem and clearly traumatised by the recent events, he strutted the length of the chaise longue with a certain ominous decorum.

Lou’s first thought was to retreat, make himself scarce but he realised that his sister needed him more than ever now. Ellie was hovering nervously around the little kitchenette, trying to make small talk to the family she hardly knew as she offered them the customary plate of cucumber sandwiches.

There had never been a time when Lou hadn’t been there for Ellie. He’d picked her up in the playground when she’d fallen, mended her broken bike and patched her up after her first boyfriend ditched her. And now he felt just a might guilty as he slunk into the living room, awaiting her sharp tongue. But it was Purdy who assaulted him as he entered, carrying a tray loaded with tea and biscuits.

Her severe expression and critical eye settled on him as they met in the doorway. Lou flinched, his culpability resurging but then relaxed as he caught the hint of mischief that played on her face.

"Well get you Lou Bannister…..so pleased you could make it."

"Sorry, Perdy……I really am. How is she?"

Surprisingly, today something about this red headed beauty, amazed him. Whether just her steadfast composure, her appropriate dress sense or maybe the way she was handling this whole bizarre affaire.

"She's fine at the moment….but not sure how she'll react when the police come calling tomorrow."

Unable to keep the shock from his face Lou grabbed Perdy's arm as she circled the grieving relatives. The tea and sympathy could wait.

"Tomorrow…isn't that just a bit insensitive? We've hardly got him buried." Lou whispered in her ear.

Abandoning the Bourbon's, Perdy ushered Lou into the chill of the hallway and turned to face him.

"It's the way things work, Lou……there's something not right about the guy's death and they've a job to do. They're going to want to interview us all so you'd better get used to the idea. After all you knew him better than most."

It was a bleak afternoon. Reminiscences of a typical childhood, a brief look at the family album and an emotional update from his mother on the findings of the post-mortem.

If anything, Ellie looked remarkably calm. The rather demure little number she'd selected suited her well, lacy and feminine it emphasised her svelte shape, the lower hemline a fitting statement for the occasion. The delicate lace at the neckline complimented her striking features as the afternoon light filtered through the bay window enhancing the false but flawless complexion.

The agony continued for almost two hours, with the dammed mynah bird continuing its elegy. Retch's mother sobbed helplessly, whilst his father stood silently by her side, his face devoid of emotion.

Lou eventually managed to round up the coats, offer appropriate condolences and usher the mourners out of the door.

“That’s just incredible,” Nette was saying as she re-positioned the frame to just the right angle on the whitewashed wall.

Lou stared intently at the small painting, detailed, animated, and strikingly similar.

“Absolutely incredible. This has to stop though…..I don’t want every little Gothic goddess Ellie encounters popping up on my screen…..”

Each stunning feature of the outfit in the framed picture mirrored the one in the photograph its colours faithfully reproduced, the unique style and cut a remarkable replica. And the face. The fair complexion, the vivid blue eyes, the tumbling auburn locks. It was all unmistakably the same.

The spotlights activated, Nette joined him and glanced at the mobile in Lou’s trembling hand. She steadied it with hers.

“And how did you make the connection?” he asked frowning. "Has she been in recently?

True she was a stunner. Very young, innocent and charming, the likeness was a remarkably portrayal of a bygone world.

Lou could just visualise the rush on Goth weekend. The veritable vampires, would be devils, the sensational steam punks…..all queuing up for the usual macabre mementos.

“It’s not recent. She’s not a customer, Lou. And she’s family… a Mc Bride.”

He moved in closer scanning the frame for a date to clarify the situation.

“Strange ….”

“It’s not a modern one Lou, some hundred years old.”

“Very strange” he reiterated.

Nette’s was calm and peaceful, yet as she spoke her voice faltered.

“Not strange, Lou……..just completely bizarre.

CHAPTER 13. Lou's story – 2014

The sudden snowfall that struck earlier in the month had given way now to a harsh frost, freezing windows and was festooning the trees with garlands of gossamer threads. In the cold days of December the B and B provided little additional comfort, its ill-fitting doors and draughty hallways chilling its occupants to the bone.

Then came the dreaded interview with the police. Two unfamiliar officers had arrived the day after the funeral. They were intending to speak to Ellie first and then the other residents, who'd known Richard from his Whitby Goth days and then move onto the Etchingham family, in their seafront guesthouse before they departed for home.

Some of the others were already packing their belongings, unaccustomed to the cruel coastal climes and seeking the comforts of a Christmas at home. So their arrival at eight thirty on the morning of the 20th was a wise move on their part.

Lou insisted on being with Ellie when they questioned her. He had to bite his tongue when they asked about Dag, though his sister's description of the weasel differed somehow from his.

How could she be so blind, Lou thought? Always looking at the world through rose coloured spectacles.

He could tell by their parting speech that they hadn't seen the back of the local constabulary and now they were heading for the Seafarer's to catch up with Gaz before the evening rush.

Lou's long term relationship with the chaise longue and its wayward springs was another source of angst and most days now he'd walk to the coffee shop for a full English breakfast then on to the Studio to meet Nette. Keeping warm was the main order of the day.

But this morning he was caught out. Still in his boxers and unshaven, his lips cracked and swollen with the wild Whitby winds and his mind still reeling from another late night revel. Frantically he rolled over to kill the ringtone.

"Hello…. "

He grimaced, eyes focussing on the list of contacts, Nette at the head.

"Lou. It's me."

"Oh Nette, what time is it?" he managed to say, before he heard the persistent rapping on the front door.

He stood bare toed in the hallway, peering through the leaded window pane. Outside leaning on the perilous porch was Nette, her face pink and rosy from running and her breath coming in short bursts. Beautiful as ever, and even more radiant than he remembered in the early morning light. Pulling the shabby throw self-consciously around his naked bits, he opened the door between them and ushered her inside.

"It's Estella Rosa…she's contacted me. You know the fortune teller I told you about, the one who Dad moved in with," she gabbled breathlessly, scurrying into the living room.

Waving a letter in front of Lou's bleary eyes, her excitement overflowed as she kissed his bristled chin.

"She's still in Scarborough and wants me to contact her there. Here I have the address."

It was some time before Lou could calm her. The eagerness in her voice and the expression on her face told him that nothing was going to stand in the way of a possible reunion with her father and no doubt Estella Rosa was the vital key to that reunion. And only when they were walking hand in hand on the windswept seafront did she display her uncertainly, speak of her reservations in finding the most important figure in her life.

"It's so strange, Lou," she was saying. "It's been years since I saw him. I know nothing of his life, where he's been living or even if he ever thinks of me."

Lou knew that he only had to be there for her, listen to her fears, hold her hand. Because now, as they walked toward the little ramshackle hut at the far end of the esplanade, he sensed she needed him more than ever.

The timber display panel below the redundant neon lights advertised -

"Clairvoyant Extraordinaire. Tarot, Palmistry - Psychic Healing."

The shabby paint on the frontage a testament to its age and confirming its bond with a bygone era, a pier end pursuit, once the ultimate tourist attraction. It looked to be unoccupied, certainly devoid of any passing trade, its neon's non-functional with only a single security lamp to lift the darkness of a December day.

"I'll wait here," Lou said, urging her forward.

"No," she said anxiously. "I want you to come in with me.

As they hesitated at the doorway, it suddenly opened to reveal a middle aged woman wearing a long flowing skirt and fitted jacket. She smiled knowingly at the two of them and stood aside to let them in.

She was a petite and shapely, surprisingly unremarkable for a woman possibly in her forties. Well preserved, with a modicum of make- up yet no striking beauty. Definitely not the typical Gypsy Rose Lee persona they'd imagined.

The interior was pleasantly warm from the log burner in the corner, with calming lights, soft music and a mish-mash of comfortable seating. Lou could feel Nette relax slightly as she observed their host and surveyed the tranquil setting.

"Estella Rosa," she said by way of introduction, indicating a small table next to the seating area and turning the music low. "I am so pleased you came."

"I wasn't sure if……"

"I'd come…." Nette uttered.

They sat down on the more formal ladder backs, upright and tense, more fitting like the mood, while Estella offered them tea and a plate of assorted biscuits.

"I heard so much about you Annette. There was never a day when he didn't say your name, look at your photos, tell me how much you meant to him."

Nette looked startled suddenly, hearing about her father in the past tense. Staring hard at their new acquaintance, Lou watched the anxiety rise in her, trying to understand the reasons for her father's disappearance and come to terms with her feelings.

"How much I meant to him?" she queried.

"When he was here…."

Lou shifted uneasily, acutely aware of the rising alarm in Nette and noted the way her hands gripped the paisley tablecloth with some vigour.

Estella Rosa poured the tea into big, tin mugs and moved the plate of biscuits nearer to her visitors. There were no airs and graces here, no frills or fancy fittings. Here was a woman living a simple life, candid and caring with a sense of justice. Lou could see it in her face as she recalled the time she'd spent with the man she'd loved and lost.

"He never really settled, to tell you the truth. I just couldn't reach him," she faltered. "It's been almost two years now since I heard from him."

There was a predictable silence as Estelle's story came to an end. Lou sensed the disappointment in Nette, the unanswered questions as she stared pensively into the flickering flames of the log burner. Then, as though Estella had read Nette's mind, she reached out and took her hand across the table, willing her to look deep into her eyes.

"I have no idea where he is, Annette but I do know he would want you to have these."

Pulling a cardboard box out from under the folds of the tablecloth she passed it to Nette.

"It's all I have left...," she lowered her gaze, blinking away tears that had appeared in her almond eyes.

"Take the box ...he would have wanted you to have everything."

Nette reached over to peel back the manila flaps, glancing momentarily at the content. Lou could tell she was desperate to search for answers, reveal its secrets, and locate the missing parts in the jigsaw of her life. But sensing it was time to leave, she quickly resealed the box and stood up to go.

"If I hear anything from him...you'll be the first to know, Annette. You can be sure of that," Estella assured her.

Lou took the precious box from Nette and reaching the cabin door they turned to say goodbye.

"It's Lou, isn't it...Lucien Bannister?"

The voice seemed to come from nowhere, rumbling round the room, an alien sound, detached from the speaker. Instantly the lights seemed to fade, the shadows lengthening, creeping stealthily up the timber walls

"Yes," Lou responded, a little taken aback.

"I have a spirit here, a persistent soul.....seems to be trying to warn you, to warn you of danger."

Estella Rosa was standing now, her eyes glazed and staring into space, her hands outstretched her face intensely animated. There was a bright light above her, highlighting the distorted face, the pattern of sheer exertion filling her being, deploying her tongue.

"She's come to warn you Lucien, to protect you and keep your loved ones safe. She says there is a shadow that falls between the two of you, an evil spirit that has already worked its wickedness and will return. Be aware, be ready for the evil. She's certain it will return."

On their return to the B and B Lou settled comfortably with Nette on the chaise longue, while Merle busied about mashing tea. His mind was still working on the recent strange encounter with the fortune teller as he watched Nette clutching the cardboard box containing the coveted souvenirs.

"Where's Ellie?" he asked casually.

It was Perdy that spoke next, blowing forcefully on her newly varnished nails.

"Oh, she's gone into town with Dag. Some tribute band, one night only…. "

Lou gasped at the sound of the lowlifes name and abruptly turned to challenge her.

"What were you thinking of Perdy? Are you completely bonkers?" Lou took the stairs two at a time. "You know he's not to be trusted."

"She's not a child, Lou. She'll be seventeen in January and you can't keep her under lock and key forever," Perdy screamed, her face flushed with anger. "And I'm not her nursemaid either."

Lou glanced momentarily at Nette, standing self-consciously in the doorway before continuing up the stairs. He stopped on the brink of Dag's room. Oh God, he dreaded to think what could happen.

"It's on the poster …on his wall. Could be the Spa or the Enterprise, not sure." Perdy's voice floated up the stairway behind him.

It was cold in there, chinks of light creeping in cast an eerie glow on the empty beds as he stood listening in the semi-darkness. The inadequate furnishings looming ghostlike in the enclosed space spooked him, a fleeting feeling that he wasn't alone. But then his eyes became accustomed and the sensation was gone.

Pulling back the cobweb curtains, he scanned the crumbling plaster walls searching for clues to his sister's whereabouts. But there was nothing to pinpoint where they'd gone, no poster, no flyers and no whiff of Ellie's familiar perfume. Tentatively he went for the drawers, delving cautiously into the very corners, fearful of disturbing the monster within. No….nothing….no hairy occupant or ticking timepiece.

"Damn!" he said out loud and rushed to wardrobe, his last chance. Otherwise he'd be working completely blind….out there in the icy streets, down shady side alleys and searching every busy restaurant and dingy bar.

He rifled the closet with a passion, till every piece of Dag's clothing lay scattered on the floor. Every item, once neatly folded, freshly laundered, immaculately stowed away now littered the dusty floorboards.

"Nothing!"

Lou stood back surveying the dark interior, angry at his own stupidity. He'd been so taken up with Nette, so preoccupied he'd never had a thought for Ellie. Pinning back the louvre doors he fell to his knees. There in the corner he could see a glimmer of light, a white glow in the darkness. Maybe a torch left switched on or a spent glow stick? He reached in, forsaking his current mission he found what looked like a manikin, a minute doll.

"My God...." he gasped.

Fitting perfectly into the palm of his hand, small but exquisitely crafted was a wax effigy. Instantly recognisable, a convincing likeness of the recently deceased Retch, his destiny cruelly portrayed by the silver pin that penetrated his heart.

Lou's knees turned to jelly, his head began to spin, fingers numb.... the obnoxious image fell instantly to the floor ceremoniously splitting in two.

Speechless, Lou's mind was racing as he dived back into the darkest recess to retrieve yet another doll. He daren't even look, there was no need.........as he stared down on the familiar fair haired figure, young, naïve and at this very moment in the very gravest danger.

CHAPTER 14. Kate's story – 1914

It seemed to be quite common place during those tense and unpredictable days at the start of the war that Kate could be found crouched in the cupboard under the stairs - arms enfolded round her young cousin; her heart thumping as loudly as his. With each explosion Edward embarked on a fit of screaming; his hands clamped firmly over his ears and his little body quaking.

German warships had launched surprise attacks on Naval Bases in Scarborough earlier that week with rising numbers of fatalities and then within hours Whitby came under fire, bringing a fresh band of casualties to the family at No. 32.

Young as she was, Kate was aware of the horrors of conflict and the devastation it was inflicting on the country and, though her father had been adamant that the war would be over by Christmas, it was looking increasingly unlikely by the minute.

There were times when Kate could easily have crumpled. Strong willed as she was and steadfast of character, she too was touched by the terrors and trauma that the war inflicted - not only on the battle field it seemed, but virtually on their very doorstep. So it was at this time, with Christmas fast approaching, that Kate began to write her diary.

1914 – The Cruel Conflict.

2nd December - 10 o'clock

Today was the day they came for Dorothy. Silent and subdued in the cold morning light she waited in the hallway for the police to arrive. I watched from my usual spot on the stairs, hidden from view imagining the empty cell where she would rest tonight. There were many questions that needed to be answered but there was no doubt about her guilt. Her confession was already neatly penned and signed, in the sight of Papa and the local constabulary, with no visible signs of remorse. I pray for her soul and a speedy recovery for her victim.

14th December – 3 o'clock

We visited our favourite patient today. His face was still pale and, although the vomiting had virtually ceased, he was still complaining of stomach cramps. I noted his fleeting episodes of confusion, the peculiar markings on his fingernails and the recent thinning of the once luxurious locks. Yet I was heartened that he recognised us, both Edward and I, eagerly reaching out to greet us.

Dr Hinton said he was responding well to the treatment and although his recovery would be slow he saw no reason why he shouldn't be up and about again within a few weeks. He asked immediately about the Springer Spaniel, aware of the constant barking in the stable block below and querying the absence of his nurse and companion Maria Hicks.

16th December – 1'oclock

Edward and I were in the playroom when they came for her. We'd barely finished our morning schooling and tidied away our books before the word came from downstairs. She went without dispute, stony faced and resolute, flanked by two uniformed officers who escorted her from the rear of the premises to help with their enquiries. In truth, at that moment my heart went out to her. Her hostile manner and stern appearance was no testimony of guilt and the prior suspicions of an imaginative minor were, to the authorities, of little consequence.

18th December – 8'o'clock

Today Anna arrived promptly to offer her services as temporary Governess. Edward and I were of course overjoyed. We entered the schoolroom with renewed vigour and the study programme was duly revised. There would be additions to our library and a review of our current subjects, which from now onward would include Arts and Craft. Mother has promised to rearrange her charity work so she can provide relief at the Studio on school mornings.

24th December – Christmas Eve

Today we wrapped our presents and lay them beneath the tree. There was one for Ma and Pa, one for Anna and a very large one we'd scrimped and saved for. The label read: - To our very special friend John Mystery. There was nothing of significance on my Christmas list. It didn't seem right, with the world in such turmoil. I lay in my bed praying for peace, the safe return of our valiant soldiers and a swift recovery for our precious patient.

25th December – Christmas Morning

Today we woke to the chime of Christmas bells from St Mary's and eagerly opened our presents. The day was remarkably calm and we were thankful for the opportunity to think of family and, for a short time, put aside the woes of war. The turkey was splendid and Edward enjoyed three helpings as well as the seasonal pudding. It was quite late as we sat in the drawing room when Mrs Dawson announced there was a visitor.

"I come to see the Gentleman."

Standing beneath the crystal chandelier Eira Munton, smelled of raw fish and there was a curious hint of seriousness in the usually mischievous eye.

"There's a seafarin' man lodging down at the Endeavour, he likes 'is fresh herring of a mornin' an' he reckons to know the gentleman...he was aboard the Rohilla."

26th December - Boxing Day

Today we gathered in the drawing room eager to hear what the gentleman from the Endeavour had to say. He was a stocky man, smartly dressed his face windswept and notched. He seemed kindly to me and his smile showed a warm recognition as Mr. M entered the room. I sent out a silent prayer that this was not just another false hope.

"Ye da' ne recognise me, James," he said.

I was sure there was some flicker of remembrance in his eye then, a connection, a glimpse of past events. It was a moment I shall never forget. The day that Mr M truly began his journey to a full recovery.

29th December – 2pm

Today we went down to the Pier for our usual walk, Mr M – ' James' - took the lead, locked in deep conversation with his new friend and council, Andrew Ferguson, Purser aboard the fateful hospital ship Rohilla. He has the kindest face I had ever seen and my belief in him has grown tremendously since his unexpected arrival on Boxing Day Eve. The glimmer of recognition that had sparked that day had prompted a flood of new memories for our dear friend James Henry Mc Bride. Mr Ferguson had the most vivid and horrendous recollections of the fateful night of the disaster and had nothing but praise for a man who, against all odds, was determined to board the ship bound for Dunkirk to tend the wounded and serve his country, despite his own debilitating health condition.

31st December – New Year's Eve 1914

I left my diary till a minute before midnight so I could put in a note on the New Year. Reflecting on the year gone by and the changing times, I find that things are not always as they seem. At times I seem so sure about things, even as they appear before my very eyes, but I have, it seems, been mistaken, I have been blind to the real truth of things. Indeed it was a grave misconception.

CHAPTER 15. Lou's story – 2014

It was the last in a line of possible hangouts - the warm ambience of the interior reaching out to draw them in - but Lou was in no mood to relax. The whole place was alive with the pre-Christmas crowd with not a seat remaining and the bar inaccessible.

"Lou, we need to go back…..they're not here."

Nette caught her breath and reached down to adjust her out of season sandals.

"Lou, about time too……you catch up with Ellie?"

They looked round to see a beaming Hathus seated at the table closest to the entrance, the rest of the crowd squashed into the adjoining seats, waving madly as they approached.

"If you can get to the bar, mine's a pint of lager mate," chirped Kalen, shaking the raven locks as he indicated two vacant stools.

Lou cast his eye round the bar. Mindful of their leader's persuasive ways, he ignored the request.

"We've looked everywhere; there's no sign of them."

Merle gave a wry little smile.

"It's ok I'm sure they're fine. Perdy's stayed back at the B and B so if they turn up there she'll call me."

"Sit down, Lou. Let me get you both one in," Hathus added.

Lou couldn't bear it. Why didn't they listen? The guy just wasn't to be trusted.

"This isn't a joke…….I told you before - the bloke's bonkers."

He grabbed Nette's arm and turned to go; his face a vivid shade of puce.

They stepped onto the pavement outside as the rain began to fall. Great droplets of water, driving against their cheeks as they slipped into the nearest doorway.

In seconds though Lou strode out again, dragging the protesting Nette behind him.

"Lou…wait."

He twisted round to see a perturbed Hathus minus his jacket - hair dripping across the furrowed brow. Hands on hips, he shook vigorously like a drenched dog.

“You’ve got this all wrong Lou. You don’t know Dag like we do……he’ll take good care of her.”

He’d be taking care of her alright, Lou was certain of that. Just like he took care of Retch and probably countless others who fell foul of his deadly trade.

“You just don’t know the half of it, Mate. I shan’t rest till I find them.”

Hathus raised himself up and took a deep breath - a look of sheer despair on his face.

“Look,” he said, “It’s our last night tomorrow - we should all get together for one last drink in the B and B. The lasses are doing a buffet and they were hoping Nette would be there.”

“I’d like that, Hathus.” she said.

“Yeah, whatever……,” Lou added. “Once we get this thing sorted.”

And then they were running, battling the elements, slipping through the narrow alleyways down to the shore.

“Where are we going now, Lou?”

“I know where he’ll be,” he began. But then, as they turned onto the square, his mobile sprang to life again.

“Perdy….right, thank goodness for that. Don’t take your eyes off her, I’ll be back in an hour.”

Reassured about his sister’s safety Lou forged on, through the windswept streets and onto Tate Hill Pier. He slipped behind a signboard outside the Lifeboat Station, dragging Nette with him into the shadows.

“Now what….?”Nette groaned, the sodden sandals rubbing her aching feet.

In the ghostly glow from the lighthouse they could make out the hunched shapes of the little bands gathered around their flickering fires. Plumes of smoke rising from their tab ends, the sound of their weary voices fused with the rhythm of the ebbing tide. The stark realities of life laid out before them, pricking their consciences, stirring sudden compassion.

“Lou!! What we doing here?” Nette whispered unable to tear her eyes from the scene before her.

It wasn't too long before her question was answered as the unmistakably familiar figure emerged from the gloom. Dressed in a grey cagoule, he stopped, as if to weigh up the weather and discarded the hood revealing his true identity. Progress slow due to the shifting sands, he made his way briskly toward the dispirited company. Far enough away to remain undetected - yet near enough to recognise the formidable features.

Spotlighted on the stretch of sand, he moved swiftly from one to the other, avoiding the random bundles of blankets that concealed younger elements of the party, his face fanned by the light of their fires. The exchanges brief, he moved swiftly on to where a man lay sprawled out on a cluster of rocks, some distance from the gathering. Addressing him, he then produced a package from beneath his coat, which Lou couldn't quite determine - handing it to the man who leaned forward - shaking his hand before showing him what appeared to be a photograph. The man stared down with a frown, pulling his inadequate coat round him. His emaciated body suddenly erupted in a wild coughing fit.

Dag stood back momentarily until the man recovered himself. The tendered snap rejected, Dag watched as the man shook his head vigorously before turning away.

"Feeding off the most vulnerable, the down and outs, it's unbelievable!!"

As they watched, the cagoule clad figure slipped silently away, leaving Lou in no doubt as to the purpose of his mission whilst Nette shifted uneasily, trying to make sense of what she had just seen.

"Lou.....what are you saying?"

But Lou didn't answer. As far as he was concerned the Steampunk scum had been caught in the act, plying his trade, apparently indifferent to the misery he caused and it was only a matter of time before the police caught up with him.

It was the day before Christmas Eve and the driving rain that had battered the coastline had ceased, favouring them with a cold but surprisingly sunny day. By mid-afternoon most of the party were ready for their departure, with bags packed and waiting at the foot of the stairs. Merle's little vanity case bulged with trinkets and souvenirs which she'd already wrapped and labelled for family and close by, a refuse sack regurgitated spent bottles and cans.

"Don't forget Lucy......last of the beers in the fridge and sorted out those old Sex Pistol tracks. Should be a good night." Hathus grinned from ear to ear, the tattooed arms rippling from the effort.

"Yeah, man," Lou assured him. "It'll be after ten....we're doing the evening shift and then prepping the veg for the big day."

Lou really couldn't have backed out of this one. They were desperately short of volunteers this week at Seafarer's with folk heading home for Christmas but Nette had agreed to lend a hand, so hopefully they wouldn't be late finishing.

They met and kissed under the Whalebone Arch, Nette excitedly filling him in about the treasures she'd found in the cardboard box - a broad smile on her face and a new sparkle in the stunning eyes. The evening passed quickly, no time to chat once they'd reached Seafarer's, filling the empty bellies and handing out the basic issue blankets.

Lou had brought an assortment of cream toffies and chocolate Santa's to the delight of the eager youngsters. His memory of the ravenous ragamuffin on that first night still haunted him.

They refilled the copper urn and stacked the dirty dishes, only managing to exchange the minimum pleasantries - conscious of the lateness of the hour. The place was heaving tonight; the dining room filled to capacity with several temporary beds squeezed into the dormitory. The atmosphere was a little livelier than usual and there were a couple of new female helpers Lou hadn't seen before enthusiastically clearing tables and handing out second helpings.

At the far end of the room Lou spied Gaz deep in conversation with one of the new recruits. Her tall willowy figure and strawberry blonde locks were somehow familiar but standing with her back to him in the crowded kitchen, he just couldn't quite place her.

Lou reached for his mobile, it must be Ellie texting again.

He stared at the screen….a random text message from an unknown source it flashed luridly in front of his eyes.

"THINGS ARE NOT ALWAYS AS THEY SEEM……..LIFE IS FULL OF MISCONCEPTIONS"

Lou clicked back to the contacts, trying to establish the caller but the screen suddenly went blank.

"Damn, should have put it on recharge."

He searched his haversack for the lead, located the nearest power point and plugged in before returning to the kitchen chores.

In seconds the iPhone was ringing again, this time on loudspeaker alerting the whole kitchen with its din.

Lou returned to answer it.

"Got to go, George," Lou said, replacing the mobile in his pocket and grabbing his jacket. "I have to pick my sister up."

"I can't thank you both enough, you know," the Vicar was saying, his ruddy cheeks a give-away of his worsening heart problems. "We're really down on numbers as you can see and lord knows how we'll manage tomorrow."

George Farmery had been Vicar in the parish for some two decades, bringing up his family alone since the death of his wife and Lou could tell he was feeling the strain.

"It's no problem, George," Lou reassured him. "We'll be here tomorrow, early… in our Christmas jumpers with a string of Mistletoe."

There was still a spark left in the elderly gentleman's eye, a quick response to humour yet Lou could tell the he was ready for retirement.

"It's no problem. There's just a few more dishes to stack and young Quilon will be back soon to finish off."

It seemed Gaz had slipped out to the Town Hall where they had been putting together Christmas parcels for the homeless and collecting warm clothing and extra blankets.

"You go, Lou," Nette said, wiping her hands on the cotton apron and returning to the dishes. "I'll finish off here."

With his mobile flashing impatiently on Ellie's text Lou grabbed his jacket and made for the door.

"If you're sure, Nette…I shan't be long and I'll come back for you," he said giving her a quick peck on the cheek.

Outside the weather was changing again, with icy pavements and biting winds to contend with. Lou cursed the despicable Dag. He never seemed to get a moment alone with Nette before he was dragged away, summoned by his sister, returned to his former chaperone duties. He was still seething as he dropped her off at the Band B following a drink at the local after a late finish. It was ten thirty when he eventually arrived back at the Seafarer's.

Standing in front of the main entrance he noticed the light flickering in the kitchen. Perhaps a faulty strip light ready to fizzle out at any moment. He'd expected Nette to be waiting in the porch, dishes washed, ready to lock up before they returned the key to the vestry.

He tried the handle, straining to see through the little window beside the porch, then knocked loudly on the door.

Suddenly from within there was an ear-piercing scream, resounding through the hollow of the interior and immediately afterward the sound of a door slamming shut. Lou hammered his fists on the on the front door again, then shouted at the top of his voice.

"Nette….."

His heart thumping in his chest, Lou sprinted down the street and through the little alleyway to the back entrance, where he could look directly into the large kitchen. The flashing strip light dazzled him as he entered the building, it's tell- tale ticking heralding its demise, like a lingering lightning strike.

"Nette…..you there?"

He could hear a faint sobbing from the far end of the room, a muffled cry that filled him with sudden fear. As he rounded the steel workstation, he dislodged a plate which hurtled down, narrowly missing his foot as it spun slowly across the floor before smashing in two.

Suddenly the struggling strip light gave up the fight and the room was plunged into darkness.

"Nette….where are you?"

Lou tensed, avoiding the fragments of splintered china surrounding him he moved into the kitchen's interior. Utilising the flashlight App on his mobile, he followed the beam.

There huddled in the farthest corner was Nette, the girl he loved, the one he dreamed of every night, arms tightly clutched around her trembling body, sobbing uncontrollably. In the dimly lit room she was hardly recognisable, her face bruised and smeared with tears, her hair matted and unkempt.

"Oh God…..What happened?"

Lou covered the floor in an instant. Trying to calm her, he wrapped his arms tightly about her shuddering form, acutely aware of the blouse spotted with blood and ripped to reveal the angry abrasions on her exposed cleavage.

For what seemed like an eternity to Lou, Nette struggled to speak. Her words coming in staccato, in tempo with her heaving chest.

“Has he gone….did, did you see him?” she sobbed.

Looking around, Lou struggled to assess the situation. Someone else had been there. Someone who’d threatened Nette, scared the living daylights out of her and then made a hasty retreat.

“It was Quilon, he was here…….he, he wouldn’t let go of me….. “

Lou put a shaking finger to her lip, drawing the stray locks from her troubled face - then held her close.

“Hush, hush…….I’m here, everything’s ok now

CHAPTER 16. Lou's story – 2014

It was gone eleven next morning when they arrived back at the B and B, having spent the night at the West Cliff - Nette falling into a fitful sleep as he watched over her from the nearby armchair.

They caused quite a stir as they entered the living room. The angry bruise on Nette's cheek was still inflamed and she looked decidedly pale.

"Oh, my God! What's happened to you?" Perdy squealed.

Lou hadn't time to explain. He'd an urgent appointment with the Devil and there was no time for delay.

"Where's Ellie……I don't want you to let her out of your sight."

Perdy frowned - her eyes flickering irritably in Lou's direction.

"She's gone down to the Seafarer's with Gaz…..something about wrapping Christmas parcels for the homeless."

Lou couldn't believe his ears. He lurched forward lost for words. He wanted to land out at someone, but he knew his anger wasn't for Perdy.

By now the rest of the tenants were filing into the hallway, Merle clutching her precious vanity case, Hathus uncharacteristically brandishing a mop and Kalen carrying out the trash can. Lou ushered Nette into the living room, settling her on the chaise longue. He kissed the top of her head, gently prising her fingers from his neck as she tried to detain him.

"Be careful Lou, please. We know what he's capable of….." she murmured, as he pulled away.

"Perdy…..I've no time to stop. I'm leaving Nette with you; she's fine now but look after her will you?"

The Seafarer's was the last place he wanted to be right now. Memories of last night's events were still painful and standing there in the cold chill of morning before the great oak doors sent shivers up and down his spine.

After finding the door locked, Lou tackled the huge Lionhead knocker - its hollow tones echoing through the ancient building with only a significant silence for response.

Then as he began to lose hope a familiar face appeared at the upstairs window, flushed and acutely apologetic.

“Oh, Lucien, there you are my boy. You’ve just missed young Garry and your sister.”

The aging Vicar looked slightly confused - the salt and pepper streaks highlighted in the wintery sunshine, his breath laboured as if he’d been running.

After all hadn’t he promised to be there first thing, peel the veg and stuff the turkey in readiness for the big day?

“He’s taken her out to lunch…….the Magpie Café I believe” he added leaning further out the top window and shouting at the top of his voice.

Lou backed away, face like alabaster and a lump rising in his throat, his whole body was shaking uncontrollably.

His mind was working overtime but his tongue was strangely tied as he sprinted down the side alley, leaving the unsuspecting Vicar dangling precariously from his vulnerable view point.

How could he have been so stupid? His own lifelong buddy, the one he’d hung out with, ogling the fit chicks and gate crashing all those wild parties. It just didn’t make sense. The one person he thought he could really rely on, his lifelong mate, his best buddy.

As he sped past the Endeavour and onto Church Street he hit the crowds. Ploughing into the maze of last minute shoppers searching for that ‘must have’ bargain, he peered into crowded shops in a vain hope he’d find Ellie there. But he couldn’t linger.

It was after twelve thirty when he called Nette.

“They’re not at Seafarer’s. George says they’re on their way to the Magpie Café. The swine’s buying her lunch would you believe. You OK, Nette?”

Hardly registering her positive response he rang off, speedily hitting the narrow harbour side by all the fish stalls and tacky souvenir stands. His stomach lurched as he took in the usually tempting aroma of fried fish from the nearby chippie. Curiously today it caused him to gag. The cry of the gulls by the quay side assaulted his ears while a little swarm of winning punters came spilling out from the amusement arcade - knocking him sideways in their exuberance.

As expected, there was a lengthy queue forming outside the popular café and as Lou approached he scanned the length of it. Tinselled teenagers, squawking kids and agitated parents all eager for a for the ultimate window seat in the famous eating emporium. Lou mounted the steps two at a time, elbowing his way through whilst pacifying a string of irate customers.

“Sir, sir……there is a queue here, Sir.”

The frustrated waiter - demoted to doorman duties - held up his hand warningly. But Lou was in no mood to delay and forcing his way through into the restaurant he dashed obliviously from table to table, searching for his sister. Convinced she wasn’t there amongst the astonished diners he turned to go as a burly, wine waiter accosted him and without a word escorted him from the premises.

Lou stood out in the street, at a loss as to what to do next. It was almost one now and the seafront pubs were clearing - filling the pavement with loud-mouthed revellers, heading toward the town centre.

He slipped past them, looking one way and then the other…....contemplating the most obvious alternatives, the all- day coffee shops, the more salubrious diners. It was a minefield, an impossible challenge, and Lou suddenly felt helpless, a useless player in a champions’ game.

He leaned against the nearest wall for support, catching his breath and feeling the rapid beating of his heart. He waited for it to subside.

“Penny for em’ mate.”

Lou hadn’t seen the vagrant squatting silently in the bank doorway, grateful for its early closure. He glanced over - taking in the rasping voice and glassy eyes that scanned his whole body with a patent envy.

“Ain’t eaten for days.”

His voice lingered on the afternoon air, the breath rancid and tainted with tobacco.

Lou knew he couldn’t stop, no time even to reply. But his heart went out to the man ….maybe one of the many unfortunate faces he’d gazed upon with compassion at Seafarer’s, or down by Tate Hill Pier. Suddenly he was on his feet, his purpose clear, his only mission to bring to justice the shameless scum that had deceived so many decent people, conned the most vulnerable of human souls and assaulted the only girl he had ever loved.

A single pound coin clinked melodically in the metal bowl as Lou gave a parting salute to the grateful street dweller and headed back into the teeming precinct.

At the foot of the hundred and ninety nine steps, Lou halted. The ancient attraction was teeming with tourists returning from their tour of the Abbey - awe-struck as they stopped to admire Whitby’s breath-taking shoreline.

Lou reassembled his thoughts. Donning his cap he negotiated his ascent, obviously a no brainer. It was then that he spotted him wedged between a spotty faced teenager and a rather large lady with a protesting Pekinese on her shoulder. Oblivious to the fleeing felon, they moved aside, unwittingly assisting his escape.

But Lou was on his trail, pressing his way steadily through the tightly knit bodies, knocked off their guard struggling to remain on their feet. But the sea snake had escaped, swallowed up in a tsunami of stunned faces and now lost from view. Peering over heads, Lou forged his way onward toward the top, ignoring the sounds of the disgruntled day trippers.

Breaking out onto the exposed churchyard Lou shuddered, tested by a strong easterly wind wafting across the headland. Stretching out before him lay the graveyard bathed in hazy sunshine prompting memories of his recent visit there. Taking the main path he suddenly caught sight of the lone figure retreating through the far gate, the familiar features and Lowry like frame moving quickly out of sight again. Lou had a fleeting memory of the school yard, the tag games and schoolboy dares - the blood-brother ties.

And then he was running again - out through the Abbey grounds and onto the scrubland, through the hawthorn hedge and out onto the clifftop.

It didn't take much to outrun him.....it never did. It was the only thing Lou had excelled at in High School and back then it had been his passion. He'd always played Gaz's side kick, the delicate one, the underdog, but if nothing else, come sports day, he could always out run him.

The distance between them shrinking, Lou accelerated, reaching his quarry in no time. He came to a standstill just metres away from the guy he had once called a friend.

"You Bastard....." he growled, discarding the sweat stained cap and running the back of his hand across his bare forehead.

Self- assured as ever, Quilon turned wild eyed and jeering. His face smeared with mud, and a criss-cross of scratches visible at the v. neck of his T shirt.

He stood motionless. The matted locks blowing in the wind behind him, provoking a veritable madman.

And then Lou pounced, gripping the powerful shoulders and wrestling him to the ground. The earth below was unyielding, ravaged as it was by the icy air currents rolling in from the North Sea. Like a scrap yard dog the beast growled, the whites of his eyes enlarged, the incisor teeth bared. The earth below was unyielding, ravaged as it was by the icy air currents rolling in from the North Sea.

Aware of the proximity of the cliff edge, he managed to throw the villain wide, one hand holding him down the other landing a punch with amazing accuracy leaving him dazed. Though wiry and lean, Quilon was no weakling, he could stand his ground, his upper body muscular, his fists keen and Lou could now perceive the hatred etched on the all too familiar face.

Then he was up, ready for reprisal, squirming free he leapt to his feet, body tense and at the ready. He swung round, fronting Lou with a vengeance; the angry scratches at his throat displaying little pearls of blood as he dived at Lou - his fist hitting the side of his head and knocking him sideways. Grimacing with pain Lou fell to the ground stunned and momentarily rendered incapable. He glared up at the raging monster, towering over him, blood meandered down his cheekbone, a stark reminder of the sheer determination of the man.

"Be careful," Nette's warning filled his head. "You know what he's capable of."

He rolled over, spurred on by Nette's image, flashing across his mind. Finding renewed strength he grabbed the fiend by his sweat stained T shirt and lifted him clean off the ground in a vice like grip.

"You won't get away with this, Quilon…….."Lou gasped as he hurled the beast closer to the gaping cliff edge. Hitting the ground his expression changed, along with his position. Scrambling to his knees, he got to his feet limping the few steps needed to reunite them, a grey mist flooding his evil eye.

Racked with fear and suddenly aware of what his former friend was truly capable of he took a step backward painfully aware that his demise could be imminent. He glanced fleetingly at the cliff edge drained of energy and then back at his assailant, desperately looking for a way out, a single strategy that would secure his survival.

At that moment Quilon lunged - his chance of remission instantly dashed. He was thrown mercilessly to the rocky perimeter, his head suspended over the rim, the bitter wind stinging his face. His head hung back. Lou surveyed the vast ocean that threatened to offer a watery grave.

"Now, you snivelling yellow belly, what you goanna' do now?" Quilon hollered, his hands threatening to release their grip on Lou's ankles.

Feeling the jagged edges of the loose rock on his shoulders, Lou held his breath, screwing his lids tight shut as a line of saliva dribbled from the corner of his mouth. Beneath him the loose stones shifted, tipping the balance and sending him further down the cliff face, his fate hanging in the balance - at the mercy of his crazy captor.

It was only a second, but it seemed like an age as he hung there ….his past life spinning before him, his time running out.

Then came the overwhelming sense of relief as he was winched up the overhang, skinning the length of his spine. In seconds he was erect, the vertigo setting in he staggered away from the rim. Then he felt the final blow. Reeling over, with a thud he hit the ground. The pain was excruciating as he struck the rocky outcrop, eyes glazed, head swimming, before the world plunged into darkness.

CHAPTER 17. Lou's story – 2014

The first thing he remembered was the utter darkness, the pounding in his head and strange faces that kept emerging before him, chanting in some foreign tongue their almond eyes frenzied and full of concern, zipping in and out of his vision. Lou groaned, tried to sit up but slipped back, into the depth of the nightmare.

Then came angels……jabbering in their marked Yorkshire twang - and miniature wise men bringing him instantly back to reality. The adults that followed were real enough, as they rapidly surrounded him, making appropriate requests for him to lie still, asking his name and where he was from.

Still disillusioned Lou sat up staring around him, as the whole horrific scenario replayed in his head. It all came back with astounding clarity. Twisting about, he glanced nervously around, scanning the headland for any sign of the monster and the nearby ridge where he'd so nearly met his fate. He rose unsteadily to his feet.

Oblivious to the pleading of his strange collection of carers who begged him wait for an ambulance, Lou stumbled forward, taking the path back toward the church. He had to find his sister, ensure her safety, save her from the evil clutches of the man he'd once considered a trusted friend.

Wasn't the house of God, a sanctuary, a place of refuge?

Surely, if Ellie was in danger, then wouldn't she head there?

He ploughed on ignoring the throbbing in his head, and the icy blast hindering his progress, seeking the cover of the hawthorn hedge before racing for the church gate. It had been left open, swinging eerily on its hinges as he approached. In the distance he could hear voices, the melodic tones of the organ and a string of excited parishioners emerging from the church door. But no one else was around the grounds and no sign of Quilon.

Lou slipped behind an alabaster angel, leaning perilously at 80 degrees, praying it wouldn't topple over before the little group had passed. Once inside the church porch, and virtually sure the last of the congregation had departed, he stepped inside.

The organ music ceased and a white haired gentleman appeared from the recess, nodding pleasantries as he collected his coat and left. Lou remained in the shadows, desperate to conceal the congealed blood and bruises.

"Well, hello. I'm so glad you've come……it's been such an eventful day and what with the Nativity Service this afternoon, I've been rushed off my feet."

Lou observed the smartly dressed young man hurrying toward him, a warm smile on his face that spoke of familiarity.

"I'm sorry, "he continued. "Lucien, isn't it!"

It was a statement not a question and even though Lou was still struggling to clear his head he had a vague recollection of the young man before him. Medium height with mousy brown hair, sensitive eyes in a broad temperate face, he blended in well with the surroundings. Holding out a welcoming hand he peered into the gloomy portico.

"Mathew Farmery - George's son," he said. "I've got Ellie in the vestry, she was in a bit of a state.......something about Garry Quilon, she said he'd got a bit heavy with her, tried to get her to go off to London with him......"

Lou heaved a sigh of relief. So Ellie was safe and sound, and thankfully, just metres away.

"I would have stayed with her but I had the Nativity to organise, a hundred and thirty under eleven's can be a little overwhelming at the best of times and Dad can't really cope alone anymore....."

Eager to be reunited with his sister, Lou stepped out of the gloom taking the proffered hand enthusiastically. The efficient young Curate gasped, scrutinizing the angry gash on his forehead and the bloodied shirt.

"Oh Heaven's, what happened...?"

In the two minute trek to the vestry Lou re-counted the events of the past few hours, the encounter with Quilon and his concern for Ellie's safety. Rounding the corner, they mounted the few steps to the entrance in double quick time. He didn't want to leave Ellie alone any longer than necessary, knowing the state she must be in and with first-hand experience of what Quilon was capable of.

A strip of light shone from beneath the door, guiding their way and inside a radio blared out, somehow disrespectful in the hallowed space.

"I locked her in....she wouldn't rest until I did. "Mathew informed him, hastily turning the key and opening the door. He entered and switched off the radio.

Then there was only the sound of a few gate-crashing sparrows circling the rafters - their little wings flapping frantically in a bid to escape. Lou's eyes left the ceiling, scanning the eight by twelve octagonal room, dotted here and there with a mish-mash of furniture, reluctant to believe the room was completely empty.

“Ellie!” Lou screamed, making his way to the fire door on the far wall that led out to the WC and throwing the door open in his desperation. There was an adjoining corridor which connected the vestry to the church beyond, locked from the inside. The key still hanging on a peg nearby.

“Where the bloody hell is she?”

“Lou…Lou, calm yourself. Let’s go back into the church, you can check with friends, see if she’s gone back to the B and B.” Mathew shouted.

Standing in the great doorway again the colossal Christmas tree church dwarfed them; its flickering fairy lights illuminating the chilly interior. Mathew hung back, taking stock.

“I can’t understand it,” he was saying.” The door was locked and there’s only the fire exit leading directly in here. “

Lou marched the length of the aisle, looking nervously over his shoulder and high up into the vaulted ceiling. After inspecting the adjoining exit, he flitted feverishly about the perimeter walls, peering round pillars, checking the Chancel. Hastily he scanned the regimental panelled pews, hoping to find some trace, just one clue that might lead him to his sister.

At the end of the aisle, he stopped - the events of the past hours suddenly catching up with him - every ounce of his strength departed, he slumped exhausted into the nearest pew.

Suddenly his mobile was active, violating the silence, shattering the peace and bringing him sharply back to reality, together with a long list of missed calls from Nette.

“She’s not come back, Lou, why didn’t you call….let us know you were Ok.”

It was all he could do to keep his voice calm, trembling he made false excuses; apologising for the bad line. Reassuring her as best he could, he hung up, promising to keep her updated.

The look on the young curate’s face confirmed his worst fears. Ellie was no-where to be found.

Where on earth could she be?

Somewhere out there, running for her life, alone and afraid. Lou shuddered.

How could he live with himself if anything happened to her?

Hadn’t there been enough misery in Whitby since they’d arrived?

Before they'd had time to speak, there was a deafening commotion from the porch, someone was hammering on the huge door, urgently turning the brass handle and letting themselves in.

Spinning round they tensed, looking at each other questioningly, apprehensively awaiting the arrival of the unexpected guest.

Lou blinked dazzled for a second by the tree lights he stared into the depths of the porch.

"You need to hurry…….it's Ellie, she needs you, now!!"

Lou squirmed. It was that low life, the stark raving Steampunk. What did he know about Ellie?

"Where is she Dag…..if you've hurt her, laid a finger on her, flogged her your filth I'll………"

The gawky, grey faced Goth, just meters away now, struggled to speak, his eyes pinpricks, like ripe blackcurrants embedded in the alabaster face.

"You've got it all wrong, Mate," he yelled, sweat pouring from his furrowed brow.

"Yeah….?"

This had better be good Lou deliberated, breaching the gap in the blink of an eye.

"I haven't got time for this Dag……If you've any idea where Ellie is, you'd better GIVE!" he yelled, grabbing the leather lapels and pinning him up against the vestry wall.

"Now steady on, Lou…." Mathew pleaded. "At least listen to him……hear him out."

"Oh I'll hear him out, Curate," he yelled at the top of his voice, one hand clutching the leather fabric, the other tensed, ready to strike.

"Perhaps he'll tell us about his vile habit? The way he makes his living, preying on the weakest and most vulnerable of our society?"

"Lou!!" Mathew circled the pair, reaching out, trying to separate them. "Remember where you are…."

Lou dismissed the warning, tightening his grip, hands cupping the scrawny neck and squeezing - the blackcurrant eyes rotating wildly in their sockets.

"And the effigies, the wax dolls, the finishing touch, hey? Just to make sure, they don't squeal!! "Lou hissed.

Suddenly Dag made a bid for freedom, adjusting his jacket he brushed himself down, smoothing the jet locks back from his pale face. He shook his head in denial.

"I've been trying to tell you, Lou. You're barking up the wrong tree......they're not mine. I just sort of confiscated them; put them out of harm's way. The voodoo stuff I found it in the cellar and the angel dust was leaking from Midnight's collar. It's not my scene man, I just wanted to keep Ellie safe that's all."

Then he made a break for the door, leaving Lou stunned, and desperately trying to take it all in.

"Look, mate......we've got to go. There's something not right here.....I seen 'em setting off....they got into a car and......"

Lou was still reeling from the shock, still desperately trying to put together the pieces. He grabbed the leather jacket arresting Dag from behind, and spun him round.

"Someone's taken her?"

Lou still couldn't quite believe it. He just couldn't come to terms with what he should have seen weeks ago, months ago, maybe even years ago.

"They don't have Ellie now; they went without her. Quilon and that girl, the one at the barbeque, with the legs and the long wavy hair. Jess I think they called her.

"Our Jessie?" Mathew whispered, his eyes widening in amazement.

Lou glanced at the young Curate, his mind tripping back to that mystical evening, the beguiling beauty who'd made a play for him, worked her magic, skilfully seducing him. The recent tete a tete at Seafarers. Quilon and the irrepressible Jessabelle, they were thick as thieves.

"Then where the hell is she?" Lou demanded.

"That's just it Lou.......they said we'd never find her, that as far as we were concerned she was dead already. Then they got into the Volvo and drove away."

"The Volvo.... they took Dad's car?"

Mathew reached the door before Dag, leading the way, shifted the heavy oaken door, before securing it behind them.

In the darkness, following the shifty Steampunk, they trekked across the churchyard, between box hedges and moss-covered memorials. Their feeble calls unanswered.

Suddenly there was a commotion within the border shrubbery and a dark shape emerged. It leapt into the air then struck the stone pathway with a protesting cry, alarmed by the human intrusion. Lou halted, dodging the obstruction as it reared up in front of them making a dash for the clump of trees ahead. Staring after the fleeing creature Lou shouted to the others.

"Oh God!! Its Midnight, Ellie's cat, her lucky charm, her pride and joy, they're inseparable."

They stared into the distance, listening for any tell-tale sound to pinpoint its whereabouts.

"It makes sense now," Mathew said. "The moggy was outside the vestry earlier, looking for food, I supposed….."

Lou didn't hesitate to take up the one and only clue they had that just might lead him to his sister.

Reaching the narrow side track, tucked away in the far corner, where he'd been before, that day of the funeral. Lou stopped by the little wall where he had lingered with Nette, while she tended the yellow roses and talked of her mother. Threading his way through the overgrown grass verges he located the grave, tended to perfection - the roses now in full bloom nodding in the moonlight. Lou could hear a soft moaning noise somewhere close by. It sent goose bumps up and down his spine as he forged on, along the rows where generations of the Mc Bride family lay, deep in their eternal slumber.

It had never crossed Lou's mind before how well respected Nette's family were, the impact they had on the local community. He moved on right to the end of the dimly lit pathway, where the grass had become a little overgrown, the brambles violating the restricted resting place, barring his way like the prince in the sleeping beauty story.

Parting the invading shrubbery he leaned forward; his breath hovering ghost like in the chill night air.

"Holy shit…..Midnight!! Whatever are you doing here?" Lou gasped.

By now the others had appeared, sweeping back the overhanging foliage, equally mystified.

"I can't understand it," Mathew was saying, running his hands down the side of the traditional tomb. "Something just isn't right……..this grave looks to have been tampered with."

Lou's mind was working overtime now, envisioning the unthinkable, fearing the worse. He scrambled to his feet, clearing the remainder of the drooping branches, to reveal the inscription.

Katherine Anne Pickering

1901 - 1972

"Cousin Kate…." Lou muttered, running his hand over the clammy marble, unable to take it in.

Abruptly Midnight sprang to life, ears erect, body braced, she swooped down, orbiting the tomb in a frenzy, her high pitched wailing filling the air.

"In God's name…..what's the varmint up to?" Mathew lunged forward, waving his arms hysterically, hoping to deter the animal.

He paused, slapping a hand to his brow, his mouth gaping in disbelief. Dag moved closer a petrified gleam in his eye.

"Get a wrench, we need to shift this slab, or it'll be too late," Lou told him.

"Now just hang on……..what are you suggesting?" Mathew shouted. "You need a court order for this sort of thing,"

"Then GET ONE." Lou bellowed, falling to his knees in desperation.

Before either one of them could respond there was a screeching of sirens, a hum of distant voices and the flickering beams of flashlights approaching. In minutes the vault was surrounded, uniformed police with panting tracker dogs winding their way into the undergrowth, flooding the area with light and staring at the surreal scene. And standing before him her face white as a sheet, was Nette, clinging to him desperately, as if she would never let him go.

"I'm sorry Lou but I couldn't stand it any longer…..I had to call them," she said.

CHAPTER 18. Lou's story – 2014

Lou rolled over - his eyelids reluctant to open and reached out to where Nette lay - her breathing soft and low. The only sound a bird pecking the window ledge outside, its wings brushing the smooth glass as it laboured. He lay still, relishing the peace of the morning, secure in the knowledge that Ellie was sleeping, alive and well, safe and sound in the adjoining room.

It had been a long night waiting for Ellie to come to in the hospital and for police officers to finish their questioning. And it wasn't until the early hours of Christmas Day when most were in full swing with the festivities that the three of them could slip away to the sanity and security of No. 32.

After a fitful sleep, the nightmares catching him unawares Lou awoke as though from a bad dream, only thankful that they'd got to her in time, and that Annette's family had agreed to an immediate investigation, so revealing the sinister secret. It was even luckier that the Ketamine dose they'd spiked Ellie's drink with, hadn't proved fatal and that black cats were indeed lucky.

According to the police report Ellie had been seized from the vestry at approximately six fifteen pm on the evening of 24th December, taken to the concealed vault and subsequently………. buried alive.

It was apparent that the burial place had indeed been violated and at precisely ten pm the investigating officers discovered Ellie's unconscious body wrapped in woollen blankets within the tomb, covered with a layer of brushwood and lying on a bed of neat Cocaine, with a street value of around one million pounds.

Lou tried to focus on Nette's breathing, the birds busy on the windowsill, the comfort of the crisp, cotton of the duvet, anything to steer his mind from the horrific events of the previous night.

"Hey there, Handsome."

The soft fingertips brushed his cheek, tenderly tweaking an ear before slipping shamelessly down the muscular torso, filling Lou once more with that familiar melting feeling. He turned, responding passionately, then suddenly withdrawing.

"You ok, Lou?"

It was only a moment before he smiled, gazing into the true, blue eyes with an appreciative smile, luring her beneath the duvet again.

"I'm fine," he said. "Just so pleased to be waking up next to you."

Today was the day he'd promised to go home. Try to make a new start, placate his parents and finally take control of his life. And yet he was reluctant to leave his new found love, the shelter of their ample bed. He was dreading the family repatriation.

It was ten thirty before they finally ate breakfast and were just about to leave when there was a knock at the door. Nette opened it hesitantly to find an ashen faced Hathus.

"We've all been so worried Lou. Mathew Farmery rang with the news in the early hours," he said, stepping inside and continuing full flow. "When you didn't come back last night, we didn't know what had happened."

It's all over the papers today of course….and we couldn't just up and leave without checking you all out. Merle and Perdy have been at their wits' end and Kalen was out till past midnight searching the bars…... She's ok, isn't she?"

As Lou nodded, Hathus clapped his hand to his head and let out an audible sigh of relief. The he proffered the expected bear hug and stood back, the colour flowing back instantly into his sensitive face.

"She's fine, Hathus. Come on in. We were just about to come over."

Following them into the living room, the gentle Giant began again.

"And Quilon of all people, I just can't believe it. Have they managed to catch up with the bastard?"

"Apprehended him at Heathrow apparently, boarding a plane to Buenos Aires - him and that Jessabelle…" Lou informed him.

"They were in it together apparently. It was her that provided the key to let them into the Vestry and Quilon who administered the rape drug."

Hathus shook his head in disbelief.

"And they actually abducted her, without anyone knowing - and buried her alive?"

"Well," Lou continued. "The Carol Service was in full swing and the organ drowned out any noise. Jessica Farmery knew the lay out of the churchyard, of course and provided all the necessary tools to prepare the plot where they concealed the consignment before taking Ellie there…."

Stopping abruptly, he turned away - a lump in his throat.

“The medics were brilliant,” Nette volunteered, taking Lou’s hand in hers. “They said we’d managed to find her before the night temperatures set in and that the drug would wear off in a couple of hours.”

“Thank goodness you’re all alright. Keep me informed Lou,” Hathus said making for the door. “It’s been a mixed bag of events but great meeting up again, mate.”

Lou patted him on the broad back, choked up and speechless again. Hathus turned at the front door, staring beyond them down the long corridor, with a wide smile.

“Well, hello Ellie…it’s real good to see you. Gave us a real fright young lady.”

Elegant in Nette’s silken dressing gown, his sister appeared to glide down the hallway, looking perfectly refreshed and stunningly beautiful. She flashed a shy smile in his direction and slipped hurriedly into the bathroom.

“Well, must be going, Lou. Perdy will be so relieved. Keep in touch you two and take care.”

In seconds Hathus had gone, pausing only for a second as he reached the whale bone arch, before donning his cap and disappearing from view.

“I’ve been reading this,” Nette said, lifting the corner of the duvet and retrieving a clear plastic wallet. “The police found it beneath the concealed drugs, stashed away in a canvas sheet. “It’s my cousin’ Kate’s diary.”

Lou looked down thoughtfully as Nette slipped it out from its protective envelope, running her hand over the dusty binding to reveal the inscription on the front. DIARY – and below, diminished with age a memorable monogram.

“Kate Annette McBride,” Lou read out loud. “She’s the one in the picture, the oil painting…….the mystery selfie. “

Nette started to flick through the crisp, yellowed pages and Lou marvelled at the meticulous handwriting, the attention to detail.

“Kate is my fourth cousin removed, and this dates back to 1914 -15, it’s almost exactly a hundred years old Lou.”

Lou slipped over to the tall Georgian windows, his curiosity aroused and pulled aside the heavy drapes. The midday sunshine streamed in filling the room with a rosy glow.

“January – 1915” Nette began.

CHAPTER 19. Kate's story – 2014

There is so much I would want to record in my new diary of 1915 but in practical terms there is so much happening in the Pickering household in this most eventful era that I have little time to record these events.

K. P.

1st January 1915

"There was much in the morning newspapers today about the sinking of H.M.S Formidable. Pa could hardly speak when the news came through. His appetite swiftly departed as he talked of all the good naval officers he knew and offered up a prayer for those whose lives were lost, their wives and children."

29th January 1915

Dorothy Jean Dobson was duly sentenced today in the Crown Court on a charge of attempted murder. The jury were in no doubt that the accused had most wilfully and deliberately attempted to take the life of James Henry McBride, an innocent and vulnerable man.

Our highly respected and capable housemaid, had always filled our childhood with happy hours and I have searched my heart, my very soul and even now as I write I cannot begin to comprehend the motive for her crime.

1st February 1915

Today was a good day. The day Pa agreed that Aunt Anna should become our new governess. Although he had had the utmost confidence in Maria Hicks in terms of our education, he no longer felt he could trust her.

He insisted we continue with Mathematics, Geography and Handwriting and the curriculum she had arranged for us. However, it was with some excitement that we began to study Fine Art and a new journey into the realms of Literature.

We start by visiting the magical world of "Alice" as she ventures into Wonderland.

2nd April 1915

It was today the telegram arrived from the Home Office that we hoped we would never see with the news that Edward's father had fallen. Henry Lloyd Pickering, had been killed during the Battle of the Marne, on the 10th September 1914. Just one of the many who'd fallen in the battlefield on the outskirts of Paris. Pa said the only consolation was, that it had been a victory for the allies.

27th May 1915

I found myself huddled with Edward, beneath the stairs again this morning, sobbing his heart out still trying to come to terms with Uncle Henry's death. It was difficult enough for him to be estranged from his mother, a small boy, with no siblings to find comfort in, but now he would have to accept that his father would never return from the war.

It was later in the day that we learned of Winston Churchill's resignation as First Lord of the Admiralty. Papa was also grieving for his lost brother and this further news was the last straw.

"Whatever shall we do without the Bulldog spirit?" he'd remarked, downcast at dinner.

14th June 1915

The events of today were, to say the least, quite out of the ordinary as literally just before the gas lights were due to be lit in the drawing room an unexpected guest arrived in the form of Eira Munton. She said she had come to see Mr M. and that she'd brought him some good news. After all 'There's nay much he does' ne see.' she remarked.

Edward and I were all ears of course but our curiosity was unresolved as the girl was duly escorted to the parlour so she and the gentleman could conduct their business in private.

16th June 1915

Today was the day our mystery guest was reunited with his father. It was a moving spectacle to see their reunion, locked in a long awaited embrace with tears in their eyes.

It seemed the spaniel had also been reunited with his master, circling the two of them and yapping gleefully.

And we were delighted to learn that his real name was 'James Henry McBride' and that he hailed from Leith, on the fringe of Edinburgh, Scotland.

5th September 1915

Dr Hinton arrived at midday, to drive Anna and James to St Mary's Church. It was a wonderful wedding, the weather perfect. We all lined up by the Abbey for the photographs, resplendent in our Sunday best.

We dined at Dunsley Hall, with twenty three guests, mostly of the McBride family, his father, brother and mother (the beautiful lady in the gilded frame) who'd travelled down from Stirling for the celebration.

CHAPTER 20. Lou's story – 2014

Nette literally glowed as she flew across the main road toward him on that joyous New Year's Day, waving the long awaited letter, that promised a change in her life, a fresh start, a new beginning.

Lou took her in his arms, lifting her clean off her feet and swung her round like an excitable child, kissing the tip of her nose and breathing in the familiar perfume.

Skipping along the promenade in front of him, hardly pausing for breath she related her news.

"I'm to meet him in the tea room on the seafront.....He's booked us a table for two at three o'clock." she was saying.

"I've to take the Coastliner straight after lunch. I told Aunt Sally and Uncle Mike and they're just thrilled."

Lou suddenly had a sense of playing second fiddle, surplus to requirements, a veritable has-been. There was someone more important in her life now, naturally and maybe he would have to step aside, blend into the background while Nette caught up with her father.

"How do reunions bide with you, Lou?" she was saying.

For a moment he wasn't quite sure what she was getting at, what was going on in that complicated mind of hers.

"You can't turn the clock back, but you can move forward Lou, look to the future. I think we both have some bridges to build, and for the moment ...." she faltered. "I think we need to go our separate ways."

Lou was speechless now, his whole world suddenly falling apart.

The radiant glow that had lit Nette's face just moments ago had evaporated and stopping abruptly on the bridge, she reached out.

Had he just imagined the feeling between them, the moments of passion, the mutual rapport, that inseparable bond?

"Cousin Kate once said.... ' Cherish the moments, the special people, the ones you hold dear because one day they may be gone, washed away with the spring tide and lost from the memory forever.'

"We need to seize our opportunities Lou, treasure our loved ones because every moment is precious," Nette said, her eyes glassy.

Then she smiled, the smile that told him he hadn't imagined it. That he was actually one of those very people she held dear.

"I envy you, you know. Your friends that is," she continued. "They're a fine bunch, Hathus and Merle, Dag and Perdy. They're the salt of the earth. And Kalen - well he's that brother you never had."

She was right of course, they'd been there for him, supported him, even when things were at their very worst.

"I've got to go now," she sighed.

"This isn't the end Lou Bannister, it's a new beginning."

Fastening the top button of his jacket ceremoniously, she stepped back abruptly.

"I've got to go now," she whispered.

"But one day we'll be together again, Lou. You'll turn around and I'll be there, just when you least expect it."

He knew it was useless to object, nor could he argue, because he knew she was right. Instead he leaned closer and kissed her, threading his fingers through the flaxen locks, aware of the salt tears coursing her cheek.

And then she was gone. He didn't call after her but turned away in search of his own future.

The sun was shining now, boldly bringing in the New Year, rising in the skies above the harbour as he walked down toward the pier, passing the little studio crammed with customers and on to the lifeboat station and the promontory beyond.

There was no one about - everyone still recovering no doubt from the midnight revels, the horrible hangovers and mulling over their New Year resolutions. Only a lone figure, kitted out for the raw coastal weather and somehow strikingly familiar. He was striding out along the pier, gazing out to sea as he went.

"Dad?" Lou called.

It was a moment before his father turned, eyes widening at the sight of his estranged son running toward him, arms open and face alight.

"Lou.....how are you?" he was saying, even before he'd reached his side.

"I had to come down, check you were all right. Mum was frantic, we haven't slept since we heard. Really missed you both."

They walked down onto the beach, feeling the rush of the wind mixed with the salt spray and talking ten to the dozen.

They stopped at the water's edge, watching the fishing boats as they sailed out through the harbour gate, the sunlight dappling the water as Lou relayed the horrors of Retch's death, the funeral, his concerns for Ellie and the horrific events of Christmas Eve. His father listened intently, relief flooding his face as he listened.

"Got a spot of work down here on the coast, stopping by to check it out on the way back. Can't do with the unsociable hours now Lou - the late night stuff. Bit of the TV documentary from now on."

Lou liked the tone of his father's voice, the way it rose and fell with the changing emotion, the light in his eyes when he talked of new ventures and most of all he loved the fact that he was actually here, in flesh and blood, talking of new beginnings.

Thank you for your purchase.

We hope you have enjoyed reading 'Grave Misconception' and are looking forward to the next Mc Bride Mystery.

We would be grateful if you could visit our Amazon product page and leave a short review.

Author Biography

Felicity Snowden is a debut Author who spent her former years reading the awesome occult of Dennis Wheatley, the English intrigue of Agatha Christie and the sheer horror of James Herbert.

Her first novel "When Dead Men won't Lie" hovers between this eclectic mix of compelling genres.

Felicity lives in West Yorkshire with her husband, son and Labrador dog. When her busy writing schedule permits she enjoys listening to music, walking, reading and spending time with her family.

Follow at facebook.com/felicitysnowdentitles

Watch out for other titles in the Yorkshire mysteries series.

Other books by Felicity Snowden available on Amazon.co.uk

'A mix of strong family bonds historical themes band the supernatural,'

'An absolutely genre-less tale which I wouldn't want to put in a box.'

'An enjoyable read, I couldn't put down.'

'When Dead Men won't Lie' Set in Morley/Drighlington, West Yorkshire in 1950's with a time switch taking you back to the Battle of Adwalton Moor.

http://www.amazon.co.uk/When-Dead-Men-wont-Lie-ebook

Printed in Poland
by Amazon Fulfillment
Poland Sp. z o.o., Wrocław

53101568R00101